Movie and Television Locations

ALSO BY LEON SMITH
AND FROM MCFARLAND

*Famous Hollywood Locations:
Descriptions and Photographs of 382 Sites
Involving 289 Films and 105 Television Series*
(1993; paperback 2001)

Movie and Television Locations

*113 Famous Filming Sites
in Los Angeles and San Diego*

LEON SMITH

McFarland & Company, Inc., Publishers
Jefferson, North Carolina, and London

The present work is a reprint of the library bound edition of Movie and Television Locations: 113 Famous Filming Sites in Los Angeles and San Diego, first published in 2000 by McFarland.

LIBRARY OF CONGRESS CATALOGUING-IN-PUBLICATION DATA
Smith, Leon.
    Movie and television locations : 113 famous filming sites in Los Angeles and San Diego / Leon Smith.
    p.   cm.
    Includes index.

    ISBN 978-0-7864-4082-5
    softcover : 50# alkaline paper ∞

    1. Motion picture locations—California—Los Angeles—Guidebooks. 2. Television program locations—California—Los Angeles—Guidebooks. 3. Motion picture locations—California—San Diego—Guidebooks. 4. Television program locations—California—San Diego—Guidebooks. I. Title.
    PN1995.67.L67 S37   2009
    384'.8'025794—dc21   99054727

British Library cataloguing data are available

©2000 Leon Smith. All rights reserved

No part of this book may be reproduced or transmitted in any form or by any means, electronic or mechanical, including photocopying or recording, or by any information storage and retrieval system, without permission in writing from the publisher.

On the cover: Beach in Marina del Rey, Los Angeles County, California (Shutterstock)

Manufactured in the United States of America

McFarland & Company, Inc., Publishers
   Box 611, Jefferson, North Carolina 28640
   www.mcfarlandpub.com

To my wife, Georgia,
who, for the seventh time,
understood and tolerated
my virtual isolation
during manuscript preparation

Acknowledgments

My gratitude goes to the Arboretum of Los Angeles County (Sandra Snider), the Queen Mary (Andy Witherspoon), and Russ Bolton, Bob Bonday, Jim Shears, Leon Smith, Jr., and Bunny Smith, all of whom greatly assisted in compiling material and photographs for this publication.

Contents

Acknowledgments vii
Preface 1
Introduction 3

Airports 5
Alleys 12
Amphitheaters 15
Auditoriums 17
Bridges/Viaducts 23
Buildings 34
Car Lots 46
Caves 50
Cemeteries 57
Churches 64
City Halls 66
Courts 81
Hospitals 93
Hotels 100
Lakes 109

Contents

Mansions 117
Movie Studios... 124
Observatories... 144
Parks 149
Piers 159
Police Stations.. 168
Railroad Stations 177
Ranches... 192
Reservoirs... 209
Rivers... 212
Roads... 215
Schools 218
Shipyards 228
Stairways.. 231
Streets 234
Subways... 244
Theaters 247
Town Squares 254
Training Centers.. 256
Tunnels 262

Index..................................... 273

Preface

The contents of this book relate the physical locations in and near the city of Los Angeles and in the city of San Diego used to film segments of motion pictures and television series. All locations listed in this publication have been identified and verified through the review of films, videotapes, still photographs taken at the time of filming, printed matter relating to motion picture and television series productions, and interviews with persons involved with the entertainment industry.

If a visit is planned to any of these locations, remember that most of the residences are occupied and that many of the commercial properties restrict entry without permission. Kindly use discretion and courtesy and do not trespass on private property or disturb the privacy of any persons.

To provide assistance to the reader, especially to visitors from outside the city of Los Angeles or the state of California, or from outside the United States, all locations are grouped by category (i.e., bridges, buildings, churches and railroad stations), all with map codes that refer to coordinates found in the respective current issue of the *Thomas Bros. Map Book* (guide) which can be obtained at the Thomas Bros. Maps Corporate Office and Showroom, 17731 Cowan, Irvine, California 92714 (714) 863-1984 or the Thomas Bros. Retail Store, 521 W. 6th Street, Los Angeles, California 90014 (213) 627-4018.

For the serious buff, a synopsis of each motion picture and television series filmed at a location is included. Additionally, a comprehensive index containing names, places, monuments, landmarks, motion picture studios, films and television series is found at the back of this book.

PREFACE

Some of the locations contained in this book previously appeared in five books written by the author (*A Guide to Laurel and Hardy Movie Locations* and *Following the Comedy Trail*, published by G.J. Enterprises in 1982 and 1984 respectively, *Hollywood Goes on Location* and *Following the Comedy Trail: A Compilation*, both published by Pomegranate Press in 1988, and *Famous Hollywood Locations*, published by McFarland in 1993). None of the listed films or television series, however, have appeared in any of the previous publications; each represents a new "find." Material on all locations is up to date and includes motion pictures and television series released up through 1999.

Leon Smith
Fall 1999

Introduction

Locations away from motion picture and television studios used for lengthy scenes and segments of film productions continue to generate an interest with fans worldwide.

Three of the most popular film locations in the United States are the cement steps of the Philadelphia, Pennsylvania, Museum of Art seen in the 1976 motion picture *Rocky*, the baseball field constructed for the 1989 motion picture *Field of Dreams* and the cement stairway seen in Laurel and Hardy's Academy Award–winning 1932 comedy, *The Music Box*. As major tourist attractions, these locations should remain intact for many decades. Other film locations, however, regularly fall victim to time and progress and disappear from the landscape forever.

Recognizing the importance of such locations to film historians, film buffs and the motion picture and television industry, I have spent more than 40 years tracking down movie locations in the greater Los Angeles area. In this book the reader will find the latest fruits of my long search. I hope it will be a valuable contribution to film history and a good read for the movie industry's many fans.

Airports

Grand Central Airport (Glendale)
Los Angeles Metropolitan Airport (Van Nuys)
Tustin U.S. Marine Corps Air Station (Tustin)

Commercial airlines began to emerge in the United States shortly after World War I but did not become popular with the public as a mode of transportation until the 1930s. This interest slowly created minor but threatening competition to the decades-old and firmly established railroad industry, both in passenger and freight service.

As air travel popularity spread, it became necessary to expand airport facilities to serve the ever-growing passenger complement and the multitudes of friends and relatives who would come to say a hello or a good-bye. Thus, the birth of the many art deco airport terminals and control towers across the nation.

As time passed and air travel became an accepted way of life, these "older" terminals were either greatly remodeled or demolished.

It was inevitable that during the years from the early 1930s to World War II, the motion picture industry would use airports for locations of various scenes in motion pictures, especially in the greater Los Angeles area as it was so close to the Hollywood studios.

The massive Los Angeles International Airport (LAX) is familiar to many motion picture and television series fans around the world as clips from that facility and its rather odd control tower appear regularly

The Grand Central Airport control tower and the west entrance to the terminal. (Photograph taken in 1995.)

on the silver screen and television sets in countless motion pictures and television series. The primary reason lengthy scenes for production companies are not filmed here is due to the crowded, around-the-clock activity both inside and outside the facility virtually every day of the year.

The "classic" airports of the 1930s and 1940s did not suffer from this perpetual activity so motion picture production companies were able to take their time filming, thus preserving on film not only a scene in a motion picture, but the airport facility itself.

Two of the most prominent classic airports in the greater Los Angeles area, airports that have not been operational for decades and, basically, only remain on film, are the Grand Central Airport in Glendale and the Los Angeles Metropolitan Airport in Van Nuys, which was the primary airport for the Los Angeles area prior to the expansion of the Los Angeles International Airport.

GRAND CENTRAL AIRPORT (GLENDALE)

The following motion picture is the earliest known feature filmed, in part, at the Grand Central Airport.

« *Lady Killer* »

In this 1933 motion picture, James Cagney stars as a theater usher who loses his job, teams with a group of gangsters headed by Douglass Dumbrille, then quickly leaves for California when the gang kills a member (Raymond Hatton) who has cooperated with the police.

Cagney arrives in Los Angeles by train at a location that will be addressed in the Railroad Stations chapter of this book.

Finding work at the National Studios as an extra, Cagney is befriended by an established actress (Margaret Lindsay) and soon rises to stardom.

Later cleared of all old charges after helping police apprehend members of the gang he was previously involved with, Cagney and Lindsay leave Los Angeles by airplane for Yuma, Arizona, to be married.

This airport is the location where Cagney and Lindsay boarded the airplane shortly before it departed for Yuma as the film concludes.

The Grand Central Airport, now an industrial complex, is located at 1310 Air Way, near the intersection of San Fernando Road and Sonora Avenue, west of the Glendale Freeway (5) in the city of Glendale, California. Map Code: 564 A2.

LOS ANGELES METROPOLITAN AIRPORT (VAN NUYS)

Twelve miles west of the Grand Central Airport is the site of the Los Angeles Metropolitan Airport which is adjacent to the large Van Nuys Airport complex in the Van Nuys district of Los Angeles.

Part of the original runway and the site of the art deco control tower of the Los Angeles Metropolitan Airport remain on Van Nuys Airport

The end of the old runway of the Los Angeles Metropolitan Airport at the terminus of Waterman Drive, looking west past the site of the art deco control tower into the Van Nuys Airport property. (Photograph taken in 1988.)

property. But two airplane hangars seen in many Hollywood motion pictures are no longer a part of the present airport and are separated from airport property by a high wire fence that parallels Waterman Drive, a narrow street that was once part of the runway of the Los Angeles Metropolitan Airport.

One hangar is located at 16205 Lindbergh Street (now demolished, with only the cement foundation present). The remaining hangar is located next door at 16217.

To motion picture history buffs, these addresses are a bit deceptive as Lindbergh Street, one block south of Waterman Drive, is now the entrance to the buildings. When the buildings were hangars in the Los Angeles Metropolitan Airport complex, however, their backs, now facing Waterman Drive, were the entrances and the part of the buildings seen in motion picture segments.

Lengthy segments of the following motion pictures were filmed at this location.

« Strike Me Pink »

Regarded by film critics as one of Eddie Cantor's worst films, the plot was Cantor as the manager of a large amusement park where he has ongoing confrontations with a gang of crooks. The amusement park is located next to the airport, which is seen near the end of this 1936 motion picture when Cantor jumps into a hot air balloon and is hoisted high above the park.

« Down Argentine Way »

This 1940 motion picture propelled Betty Grable to stardom and was the first film appearance of the "Brazilian Bombshell," Carmen Miranda. The plot centers on an Argentine horse breeder (Don Ameche) who marries an American woman (Grable) and introduces her to his culture, a culture to which she has great difficulty adjusting. The airport is said to be in Buenos Aires, Argentina, when Grable arrives to meet Ameche.

« Heavenly Days »

In this World War II entry of the "Fibber McGee and Molly" motion picture series (1935–1952), the famed radio comedians go from their home located at the fictional address of 79 Wistful Vista in an unknown town to Washington, D.C., in 1944 to help run the U.S. Senate. This airport is an airport outside their town where they board an airplane en route to the nation's capital.

The art deco control tower seen in these motion pictures was demolished in the 1960s. Its site is at the west end of Waterman Drive on Van Nuys Airport property.

The runway seen in these motion pictures is now Waterman Drive and extends beyond the roadway's west terminus into the Van Nuys Airport complex.

10   *Airports*

The east blimp hangar of the Tustin USMC Air Station, a frequent location in *This Man's Navy* (1945). (Photograph taken in 1998.)

These Los Angeles Metropolitan Airport locations are along or near Waterman Drive, west of Woodley Avenue and west of the San Diego Freeway (405). Map Code: 531 F3.

Tustin U.S. Marine Corps Air Station (Tustin)

The Tustin U.S. Marine Corps Air Station in Tustin, California, which is located in Orange County immediately south of Los Angeles

County, is a large military facility that includes an operational helicopter base. Within this facility are the largest wooden structures in the world. They are blimp hangars, each 1100 feet long, 300 feet wide and 170 feet high.

Both opened in 1942 and immediately provided housing and service for the many U.S. Navy blimps that patrolled the West Coast during World War II.

This facility is a location for many scenes in the following motion picture.

« *This Man's Navy* »

A typical World War II entry, this 1945 military motion picture stars Wallace Beery as a crusty old Navy man who takes a liking to a much younger sailor (Tom Drake) and treats him like a son.

Both are assigned to the blimp arm of the Navy and patrol the coastline in search of enemy submarines.

This facility (the blimp hangars) is a primary location throughout this film.

The Tustin U.S. Marine Corps Air Station is located west of East Edinger Avenue, between Red Hill Avenue and Jamboree Road in Tustin, California. Map Code: 830 A7, B7 & C7 and 860 A1&2, B1&2 and C1&2 (Riverside/Orange Counties Map Book).

Alleys

Clay Alley (Los Angeles)

Alleys are generally found in the older neighborhoods of Los Angeles as, during the construction boom in Southern California that began shortly after World War II, builders found it very profitable to greatly reduce them in the residential areas. Alleys, however, continued to be an integral part of established and newly-constructed business districts throughout the city due to the necessity to maintain delivery access to buildings lining busy main streets.

Motion picture production companies began using alleys for scenes as far back as the silent era and continue to do so today.

CLAY ALLEY

In the downtown area, Clay Alley was the last street in the city of Los Angeles to have a cobblestone surface, which was installed in the 1880s. This lingering bit of local history disappeared in the 1970s when the stones were removed and the alley resurfaced with asphalt. One decade later, the alley was demolished when an apartment complex was constructed between the 2nd Street and 3rd Street tunnels facing Hill Street.

ALLEYS 13

The site of Clay Alley, beyond the parking area and to the rear of the Wells Fargo Center at 235 S. Hill Street. (Photograph taken in 1998.)

The alley, whose length was but two blocks, running between 2nd Street and 4th Street, paralleling Hill Street, on the west side of Hill Street, was seen for decades in many film documentaries promoting tourism as it ran directly under the world famous Angels Flight, the world's shortest railway, once located on the south side of the 3rd Street Tunnel. It is now located one block south, near 4th Street.

This alley was a primary location in several scenes of the following motion picture.

« *The Glenn Miller Story* »

This 1954 musical/biography traces the life of the famous bandleader from near poverty on the streets of Los Angeles to his meteoric rise to musical heights with his world-famous band, and then to his tragic death in an airplane crash over the English Channel near the end of World War II in Europe.

The film opens on Clay Alley as Miller (James Stewart) comes to a pawn shop, the East Los Angeles Loan Company, owned by W. Kranz (Sig Ruman) to redeem his trombone, a musical instrument Miller had hocked many times for money to make ends meet.

The alley is also the location in the film where Miller meets his friend and fellow musician (Harry Morgan) who seems to have a greater interest in automobiles than music.

These scenes were filmed in the alley directly above the 3rd Street Tunnel (the pawn shop) and between the 3rd Street Tunnel and the 2nd Street Tunnel (automobile segments).

The site of Clay Alley is east of the Harbor Freeway (110) in downtown Los Angeles. Map Code: 634 F4.

Amphitheaters

Hollywood Bowl (Hollywood)

HOLLYWOOD BOWL

The most famous amphitheater in the United States is the Hollywood Bowl, primarily attributable to its location in the film capital of the world and due to its use in many motion pictures and short subjects whose plots revolve around a variety of performances at this scenic site.

Situated in the Hollywood Hills, this area was often a location for motion pictures, especially Westerns prior to 1919 when the idea for local culture was born and the first of many structures was built on this site.

The present amphitheater was constructed in 1929 and slightly modified over the years to provide acoustical enhancement.

A lengthy scene of the following motion picture was filmed at this location.

« Anchors Aweigh »

Frank Sinatra and Gene Kelly star in this 1945 musical as two sailors who are awarded Silver Stars for wartime bravery. The ceremony takes place aboard a ship in San Diego with Jose Iturbi directing the U.S. Navy band.

16   AMPHITHEATERS

The Hollywood Bowl and the approach Frank Sinatra and Gene Kelly took to the stage in *Anchors Aweigh* (1945). (Photograph taken in 1986.)

Given four days' leave, Sinatra and Kelly head for Hollywood where they meet a fledgling actress (Kathryn Grayson) and promise her a singing audition with Iturbi, a man they have never met.

Desperate to get Grayson the audition, the two learn that Iturbi is rehearsing at this site. Refused entrance because of strict rules, they hurry into the hills behind the Bowl, but miss Iturbi who concludes his rehearsal before they can scramble down the aisles to the stage.

The Hollywood Bowl is located at 2301 N. Highland Avenue, north of Franklin Avenue and west of the Hollywood Freeway (101) in Hollywood. Map Code: 593 E3.

Auditoriums

Shrine Auditorium (Los Angeles)
Olympic Auditorium (Los Angeles)
Pasadena Civic Auditorium (Pasadena)

Today's auditoriums are constructed primarily as sports arenas to accommodate the ever-growing variety of indoor sporting events. In decades past, these huge buildings were constructed for political conventions and gatherings for various civic affairs.

Most of the older auditoriums across the United States have been demolished and replaced with those of modern architecture and upgraded facilities to accommodate today's needs. Some, however, still exist and have a wealth of local history, especially those in the Los Angeles area, many of which have been the locations of motion pictures and television series segments.

The following motion pictures and television series were filmed at these older buildings.

SHRINE AUDITORIUM (LOS ANGELES)

The Shrine Auditorium, a Los Angeles landmark for seven decades, was designed by the noted architect G. Albert Lansburg and completed

18   *Auditoriums*

The Royal Street entrance to the Shrine Auditorium, the entrance utilized for the Academy Awards ceremonies and the entrance seen in the listed films. (Photograph taken in 1988.)

in early January 1926. It ranks as the largest theater in the United States, with a seating capacity of 6,700, and is Los Angeles Historic-Cultural Monument #139.

The interior and exterior of the auditorium are primary locations in the following motion picture.

« *Naked Gun 33⅓: The Final Insult* »

The third entry in the *Naked Gun* series, this 1994 motion picture stars Leslie Nielsen as Lt. Frank Drebin, who is now in retirement, but is lured back into the police squad to handle one more case, a fiendish plot to bomb the upcoming Academy Awards ceremony.

The love of Drebin's life, Priscilla Presley, is incensed that he has returned to the Los Angeles streets and is horrified at the scrapes he becomes involved in as he tumbles and stumbles his way through the Awards ceremony to eventually prevent the expected catastrophe.

The Academy Awards ceremony scenes in this motion picture (some were actual footage of past Academy Awards ceremonies that are regularly held at this location) were filmed inside and outside the auditorium.

As a note of interest, this auditorium is the location Senator John F. Kennedy made a political speech to an overflow crowd in 1960 en route to his election as the 35th president of the United States.

The Shrine Auditorium is located at the intersection of Jefferson Boulevard and Royal Street, across Jefferson Boulevard from the vast campus of the University of Southern California (USC), west of the Harbor Freeway (110). Map Code: 674 B1.

OLYMPIC AUDITORIUM (LOS ANGELES)

When dedicated on August 5, 1925, the Olympic Auditorium, with a seating capacity of 15,300, became the largest boxing arena in the western United States.

Eight decades later, this auditorium remains open and features many athletic events annually, primarily boxing and wrestling matches.

The interior and exterior of this building are frequently used as locations for motion pictures and television series segments.

The Grand Avenue entrance to the Olympic Auditorium. (Photograph taken in 1988.)

« *Virtuosity* »

An unpleasant look at society's future, this 1995 motion picture takes place in Los Angeles and stars Denzel Washington as an ex–Los Angeles police officer who is in prison for murder, but released as he is the only person who can track down a computer-generated cyborg (Russell Crowe) who has been programmed with information gleaned from the world's worst serial killers.

The exterior and interior of this auditorium are in one lengthy scene wherein Crowe storms into a crowd watching a wrestling match and kills at random.

« Man on the Moon »

In this 1999 motion picture, Jim Carrey stars as comedian Andy Kaufman, who struggles to make it big in the entertainment industry, dying in 1984 at age 35 as the result of lung cancer.

During filming in 1998 at this auditorium, Carrey was recreating a wrestling scene between Kaufman and pro wrestler Jerry Lawler. Lawler, who was contracted to appear with Carrey in the scene, suddenly attacked Carrey, resulting in Carrey's being taken to a hospital for treatment.

Ironically, Lawler, performing a "piledriver" move on Kaufman during a wrestling match 16 years earlier, also caused Kaufman to be hospitalized.

The Olympic Auditorium is located at 1801 Grand Avenue, near downtown Los Angeles, south of the Santa Monica Freeway (10) and east of the Harbor Freeway (110). Map Code: 634 D6.

PASADENA CIVIC AUDITORIUM (PASADENA)

North of Los Angeles is the lovely city of Pasadena, which hosts the magnificent Rose Parade and the traditional Rose Bowl football game each New Year's Day, and also boasts the magnificent Pasadena Civic Auditorium, the location of many civic events and the primary location of the following motion pictures.

« Divine Madness »

This 1980 motion picture, filmed primarily at this location, is all Bette Midler, centering on a concert wherein she does a retrospective of her career, her music and many comical characters she has portrayed over the years in concerts.

« 10 »

The plot of this 1979 motion picture centers on a Hollywood musician (Dudley Moore) who becomes infatuated with a beautiful woman (Bo

22 *AUDITORIUMS*

The Pasadena Civic Auditorium. (Photograph taken in 1988.)

Derek) and slowly drifts into a fantasy world wherein he imagines himself to be Derek's lover.

The Pasadena Civic Auditorium is part of a downtown Pasadena complex that includes a conference building and an exhibition hall located at 300 East Green Street, between Los Robles Avenue and Arroyo Parkway, south of the Foothill Freeway (210). Map Code: 565 J5.

Bridges/Viaducts

1st Street Viaduct (Los Angeles)
4th Street Viaduct (Los Angeles)
6th Street Viaduct (Los Angeles)
Glendale-Hyperion Viaduct (Los Angeles)

All metropolitan areas in the United States located in hilly terrain and near rivers, streams and creeks have an assortment of bridges or viaducts. A bridge and a viaduct have the same basic function: each is a means of surmounting otherwise impassable terrain. A bridge is a structure carrying a pathway or roadway over a depression or obstacle. A viaduct is a bridge resting on a series of concrete arches, having high supporting towers or piers.

The city of Los Angeles has many bridges crossing the Los Angeles River, which courses through a wide cement channel and which, two centuries ago, was the primary source of nourishment for local Indians. Today, during the many months without rain, little water flows down it toward the Pacific Ocean. But during the weeks and sometimes months of rainy periods, it serves the city and surrounding communities well, acting as a giant storm drain. Oddly and historically, it is the only river in the United States whose course was established by a city ordinance.

Hollywood motion picture production companies found the Los Angeles bridges and viaducts to be desirable locations as far back as the 1920s. The young television industry followed suit in the 1950s, and location filming continues to this day.

The 1st Street Viaduct, looking west toward downtown Los Angeles. (Photograph taken in 1998.)

1st Street Viaduct (Los Angeles)

Beginning in the downtown Los Angeles area, the 1st Street Viaduct is a long cement structure with distinctive and decorative columns that once bordered the old Santa Fe Railroad Station, which was replaced as the city's primary transit location when in 1939 a railroad station that still serves the Southern California area, Union Station, opened.

The site of the Santa Fe Railroad Station (see next page), immediately south of the 1st Street Viaduct, is now occupied by the Light Rail–Metro Rail Maintenance Facility. The address is 284 S. Santa Fe Avenue.

The following motion pictures were filmed, in part, at or near the Santa Fe Railroad Station with the 1st Street Viaduct in all of the primary scenes.

BRIDGES/VIADUCTS

The long building (right of photograph) is the site of the old Santa Fe Railroad Station. The building (left of photograph) stands on the passenger loading/unloading area seen in the films. (Photograph taken in 1998.)

« The Abyss »

The plot of this 1989 motion picture revolves around the involvement of an oil rig crew attempting to rescue a sunken nuclear submarine and the very surprising underwater discovery of alien life.

« Stop! or My Mom Will Shoot »

In this 1992 film, Sylvester Stallone and Estelle Getty star as a cop and his outspoken mother on a mission to clean crime from the streets of Los Angeles. The viaduct and nearby Santa Fe Avenue are seen in one segment as Getty buys a gun and in another segment where Stallone and Getty are in a shootout with a gun dealer.

« The Last Action Hero »

The plot of this 1993 film centers on a boy (Austin O'Brien) who has a "magic ticket" that propels him through the huge screen in a movie theater and into an action movie that stars Jack Slater (Arnold Schwarznegger). The viaduct is seen in one action segment in which Slater's car crashes through the railing.

« The Invaders »

The viaduct is in one scene of this 1995 film that centers on an ex-convict (Scott Bakula) who learns of an alien invasion of Earth but can't convince authorities.

« Money Talks »

A Los Angeles television newsman (Charlie Sheen) gets mixed-up with a ticket-scalping street hustler (Chris Tucker) who works in a car wash and is arrested for a murder he didn't commit.

Tucker claims to be the son of singers Vic Damone and Diahann Carroll, a claim few believe.

Many Los Angeles locations, including the viaduct, are seen throughout this 1997 motion picture.

The 1st Street Viaduct is located between Santa Fe Avenue and Mission Road in downtown Los Angeles. Map Code: 634 H4.

4TH STREET VIADUCT (LOS ANGELES)

Immediately south of the 1st Street Viaduct is the 4th Street Viaduct, a cement structure with its own distinctive features, the most prominent ones being at its west terminus where it arches over Santa Fe Avenue, a main north/south traffic artery that services hundreds of transport trucks on a daily basis.

With its unusual cement configuration, the viaduct has proved to be a favorite location for many production companies.

The following motion pictures and television series, in part, were filmed at this location.

« *The Naked Gun: From the Files of Police Squad* »

This 1988 motion picture, based on the television series *Police Squad* (1982), features the hilarious antics of Lt. Frank Drebin (Leslie Nielsen) around Los Angeles during his assignment to guard and protect the Queen of England.

A spectacular vehicle chase and crash takes place on Santa Fe Avenue at the viaduct.

« *Police Academy 6: City Under Siege* »

The screwball police academy graduates, led by Bubba Smith, are on the city streets again to put an end to a crime wave in this 1989 motion picture. A lengthy vehicle pursuit near the conclusion of this motion picture comes down Santa Fe Avenue and under the viaduct.

« *An Innocent Man* »

This 1989 motion picture features Tom Selleck as an airline mechanic who is framed by the police on a drug charge. While in prison he learns a way to get revenge. The viaduct is a primary location for several scenes.

« *In the Line of Duty: Kidnapped* »

The FBI conducts an intensive manhunt through Los Angeles for a dangerous criminal (Dabney Coleman) who has kidnapped two boys from their Beverly Hills homes. Many Los Angeles locations are seen in this 1995 motion picture, the primary ones being Santa Fe Avenue and the viaduct.

« Fast Company »

A television reporter (Ann Jillian) and her husband (Tim Matheson), a police detective, become rivals as they attempt to solve the murder of a call girl. A horrific vehicle explosion on Santa Fe Avenue under the viaduct is the primary scene in this movie, which is filmed on many Los Angeles streets.

The plot of this 1995 motion picture is similar to the 1938 motion picture of the same title that starred Melvyn Douglas and Florence Rice as a married couple attempting to solve the murder of a book dealer. A sequel, entitled *Fast and Loose*, was released in 1939.

« A Face to Die For »

In this stark drama, a severely disfigured woman (Yasmine Bleeth) is imprisoned for a crime she didn't commit. After her release she undergoes extensive plastic surgery, assumes a new identity, then gets revenge on the man (James Wilder) who caused her imprisonment. This 1996 motion picture opens and closes on Santa Fe Avenue under the viaduct.

« Independence Day »

Will Smith stars as a fighter pilot and Bill Pullman a computer whiz who help fight off the invasion of 15-mile-wide spaceships from another planet when aliens suddenly invade Earth in this 1996 motion picture.

The viaduct and Santa Fe Avenue are the locations from which a Los Angeles crowd is watching one of the spaceships.

« The Rockford Files: If the Frame Fits »

In yet another motion picture based on the very popular television series *The Rockford Files* (1974–1980), James Garner reprises his role in this

Opposite: **The 4th Street Viaduct, looking east toward the Los Angeles River. (Photograph taken in 1998.)**

1996 release as the Los Angeles private investigator Jim Rockford. In one lengthy scene, Garner arranges a meeting under the viaduct.

« *The Twilight Zone* » *(1959–1964/1985–1987)*

In this 1986 episode of the lengthy television series, a small brick building located in Memphis, Tennessee, where Elvis Presley worked in 1954 is on the west side of Santa Fe Avenue, immediately north of the viaduct.

The 4th Street Viaduct is located between Santa Fe Avenue and Mission Road in downtown Los Angeles. Map Code: 634 H5.

6TH STREET VIADUCT (LOS ANGELES)

The next bridge south of the 4th Street Viaduct is the 6th Street Viaduct, a very distinctive structure with its curved iron arches that cascade high above its support sections.

« *The Mask* »

This 1994 comedy motion picture's central character, Jim Carrey, is a bank clerk who has absolutely nothing going for him in a duller-than-normal life. This boring situation suddenly changes when he finds a mask in a heap of floating trash in a river.

Later, when Carrey reluctantly places the mask on his face, he suddenly becomes a cartoon character right out of the motion picture cartoons of the 1940s and lives his most outlandish fantasies.

At the conclusion of the film, Carrey tosses the mask from a bridge into a river far below, hoping he will return to a more normal way of life.

This bridge is the 6th Street Viaduct. The city in the background and the very wide river below the viaduct, however, are digital computer effects.

Opposite: **The 6th Street Viaduct, looking east toward the railroad yards and the Los Angeles River. (Photograph taken in 1998.)**

As a note of interest, directly under the viaduct is an access tunnel from Santa Fe Avenue to the Los Angeles River, a tunnel made famous in the 1954 motion picture *Them!* (addressed in the Tunnels chapter of this book).

« *Perfect Alibi* »

The widow (Teri Garr) of a policeman teams with a Los Angeles police detective (Hector Elizondo) to investigate a series of murders by a French nanny (Lydie Denier) in this 1994 motion picture.

In a wild ride across the 6th Street Viaduct to impress her lover (Alex McArthur), Denier cuts in and out of traffic and even drives in the opposite lane, barely missing oncoming cars and trucks.

The 6th Street Viaduct is located between Santa Fe Avenue and Mission Road in downtown Los Angeles. Map Code: 634 H6.

GLENDALE-HYPERION VIADUCT (LOS ANGELES)

The Los Angeles River continues north from the downtown Los Angeles area for several miles until it veers west toward Universal City and the huge Universal Studios complex, passing under many bridges and viaducts, one being the Glendale-Hyperion Viaduct that not only spans the Los Angeles River, but the Golden State Freeway (5) as well.

The following motion pictures were filmed, in part, on or near this viaduct.

« *In Society* »

This 1944 motion picture features Bud Abbott and Lou Costello as plumbers who are called to a mansion to fix a minor leak in a bathroom but instead virtually destroy the magnificent structure.

BRIDGES/VIADUCTS   33

The Glendale-Hyperion Viaduct, looking north toward the city of Glendale. (Photograph taken in 1995.)

Later in the film, the two comics are involved in a hectic car chase through Los Angeles streets. The film footage from W.C. Fields' *Never Give a Sucker an Even Break* (1941) was used with the exception of close-ups of Abbott and Costello which replaced those of Fields.

« *Race Against Time: The Search for Sarah* »

The owners of a motel (Patty Duke and Richard Crenna) desperately search for their daughter, who was kidnapped during a carjacking.

This viaduct is a location near the motel and is seen several times in this 1996 film.

The Glendale-Hyperion Viaduct is #164 in the city of Los Angeles' Historic-Cultural Monuments listing. It is bounded by Greensward Road on the north, Ettrick Street on the south, and is in the city of Los Angeles, just west of the city of Glendale. Map Code: 594 D2.

Buildings

Bradbury Building (Los Angeles)
Anjac Building (Los Angeles)
Spring Street Towers (Los Angeles)
749 E. Temple Street (Los Angeles)
Pico House (Los Angeles)
Goodyear Tire and Rubber Plant (Los Angeles)

Over the decades, many buildings have been used by motion picture and television production companies for filming in the Los Angeles area. Most still exist nearly one century later. Some, however, have been demolished as time and progress have taken their toll.

The following motion pictures and television series were filmed at a wide variety of buildings in the greater Los Angeles area.

BRADBURY BUILDING (LOS ANGELES)

One of the most photographed and visited buildings in downtown Los Angeles is the Bradbury Building. Completed in 1893, the five-story brick structure is a tribute to the city's Victorian past. Its ceiling is capped by a 50-by-120 foot glass skylight that allows sunlight to flow through an interior of brick, tile and ornamental iron. A main attraction of the building and a tourist delight are two open cage elevators that operate in exposed shafts, transporting persons to iron-grilled balconies that provide access to a wide variety of offices.

The ornate architecture of the building, allowing one to step back in time immediately after passing through one of two entrances, quickly became a favorite location for motion picture and television series production companies.

The following motion pictures and television series were filmed, in part, at the Bradbury Building.

« *The Indestructible Man* »

Lon Chaney, Jr., stars in this 1956 motion picture as "Butcher" Benton, a man awaiting execution in prison who swears to kill three men who framed him.

After he is executed, Chaney is taken to a San Francisco mortuary and then secretly sold to a local doctor who is experimenting on a cure for cancer and needs a body for research. One element of this experiment is the bombardment of Chaney's body with 300,000 volts of electricity, which not only accidentally brings him back to life but makes him virtually indestructible.

The Bradbury is seen many times throughout the film as an office building that housed the office of one of the men who framed Chaney.

The historic Angels Flight, the world's shortest railroad, is also seen many times in this film and will be addressed in the Railroads chapter of this book.

The site of a cement stairway located near Angels Flight, at the intersection of 3rd and Hill Street in downtown Los Angeles, is also seen in several scenes of this film and in several other major motion pictures. It will be addressed in the Stairways chapter.

« *Amelia Earhart: The Final Flight* »

Diane Keaton portrays the legendary flier in this 1994 motion picture that explores her life from youthful dreams of flying to her 1937 disappearance near Howland Island in the Pacific Ocean as she attempted to circle the earth at the equator in a twin engine Lockheed Electra 10-E airplane.

The building is seen in several segments of the film.

« A Burning Passion »

The Bradbury Building is seen often in this 1994 motion picture that centers on the love life of author Margaret Mitchell (Shannen Doherty) in Atlanta, Georgia, from 1918 to 1937. Mitchell wrote the immortal novel *Gone with the Wind*, which was made into the 1939 motion picture of the same title, starring Clark Gable and Vivien Leigh.

As a note of interest, Gable's only child, John Clark Gable has a small role in this Margaret Mitchell film, appearing as an Army officer named Terry.

« Greedy »

Michael J. Fox stars in this 1994 comedy about an elderly scrap-metal millionaire (Kirk Douglas) who outsmarts his greedy relatives who will stop at nothing to inherit his fortune.

The Bradbury Building is an apartment building in the final scenes of this motion picture, as Douglas informs Fox that he will get the fortune instead of the relatives.

« Wolf »

The building is an old building in New York City in this 1994 motion picture starring Jack Nicholson as a Manhattan editor who turns into a werewolf.

Michelle Pfeiffer is Nicholson's love interest.

« Donor Unknown »

A Beverly Hills, California, insurance executive (Peter Onorati), in desperate need of a heart transplant, receives one in this 1995 motion picture. He later learns, however, that the donor is an illegal alien who was purposely killed so his heart could be used in the transplant. This building is in several scenes throughout the film.

BUILDINGS 37

The Bradbury Building, looking south on Broadway from 3rd Street. (Photograph taken in 1998.)

« Murder in the First »

Christian Slater stars as a young lawyer who defends an Alcatraz inmate (Kevin Bacon) accused of murder in the 1930s.

The Bradbury is the law office of the public defender where Slater works, in this 1995 motion picture.

« On the Line »

Los Angeles Police Department detectives (Linda Hamilton and Jeff Fahey) investigate a series of bank robberies committed by a group of teenagers. Four Los Angeles locations are used in various scenes throughout this 1998 movie. The Bradbury is a bank building near the end of the film; the last bank the gang robbed before their capture after a shoot-out in front of the edifice as they crossed Broadway, heading into the Grand Central Market.

« *Front Page (1993-1994)* »

The building is seen repeatedly in segments from this prime-time weekly investigative series addressing major stories and a variety of topical issues that feature five young reporters, one being Ron Reagan, the son of former president Ronald Reagan.

As a note of interest, the Bradbury Building houses Ross Cutlery, a business specializing in the sale of knives where Orenthal James Simpson was suspected of buying a knife shortly before the 1994 murders of Nicole Brown and Ron Goldman.

This building is #6 in the city's Historic-Cultural Monuments listing and is located on the southeast corner of 3rd Street and Broadway in downtown Los Angeles, east of the Harbor Freeway (110). Map Code: 634 F4.

ANJAC BUILDING (LOS ANGELES)

Seven blocks south of the Bradbury Building on Broadway is a building used as a location in the following motion picture.

« *Predator 2* »

The creature from outer space featured in the movie *Predator* (1987) returns in this 1990 motion picture, this time seven years in the future, in 1997 Los Angeles.

A Los Angeles police lieutenant (Danny Glover) stalks and is stalked by the creature, who in one scene, perches itself atop this building as it stalks Glover.

The giant perch is the Anjac Building, located at 1031 S. Broadway in downtown Los Angeles. Map Code: 634 E5.

BUILDINGS 39

The Anjac Building, 1031 S. Broadway in downtown Los Angeles.
(Photograph taken in 1998.)

Spring Street Towers (Los Angeles)

Three blocks north and one block east of the Anjac Building is one of the city's perennial motion picture and television series locations. It is the historic Spring Street Towers, a 12-story structure dedicated in 1920 and the former headquarters for the Bank of America. Since its closing, the building has been used primarily as a setting for bank segments in a variety of films.

« *The Mask* »

The plot of this 1994 motion picture was previously addressed in the Bridges chapter of this book.

Bank clerk Jim Carrey becomes a cartoon character when he places a mask on his face. In this film, he is employed at the Edge City Savings Bank and assigned to the New Accounts Department.

All bank scenes were filmed in the interior and the exterior of the building.

The Spring Street Towers building is located at 650 S. Spring Street in downtown Los Angeles. Map Code: 634 F5.

749 E. Temple Street (Los Angeles)

Seven blocks north and seven blocks east of the Spring Street Towers is a small 1920s building that has been a motion picture location several times in the past eight decades. Many businesses operated out of it over the years, and it now houses a vehicle repair garage.

Scenes from the following motion picture were filmed at and in this building.

Opposite: The Spring Street (west) entrance to the Spring Street Towers seen in *The Mask* (1994). (Photograph taken in 1998.)

The building located at 749 E. Temple Street in downtown Los Angeles, seen in *Eye for an Eye* (1996). (Photograph taken in 1998.)

« *Eye for an Eye* »

  This building is a garage at "5th and Temple" in this 1996 film that relates the determined efforts of a mother (Sally Field) to bring to justice the man (Kiefer Sutherland) who raped and murdered her daughter and was released by the court because the police obtained evidence illegally.
  Field came to this building to meet a man (Philip Baker Hall) to plan Sutherland's murder.
  This building is located at 749 E. Temple Street, south of the Hollywood Freeway (101) in downtown Los Angeles. Map Code: 634 H4.

PICO HOUSE (LOS ANGELES)

Four blocks west and two blocks north of 749 E. Temple Street is the Pico House, a magnificent three-story building located at 410 N. Main Street, on the south boundary of historic Plaza Park, a Los Angeles landmark since the 1880s and a major tourist attraction.

The building was originally known as the Pico House from 1869 to 1870. It then became the National Hotel in 1892 and remained so until 1920 when the hotel closed, again reverting to its present name.

The following television series episode was filmed at this location.

The north entrance to the Pico House in Plaza Park in downtown Los Angeles, a location in *Amazing Stories* (1985). (Photograph taken in 1998.)

« Amazing Stories »
(1985–1987)

This building is said to be just outside the Alamo in San Antonio, Texas, in the 1985 "Alamo Jobe" episode of this television series.

A teenager (Kelly Reno), fighting with Col. Travis and Davy Crockett at the final battle in 1836, is given a letter by Col. Travis to be taken to General Leffert requesting help.

As soon as Reno steps through the entrance, he enters 1985 San Antonio and a park (the Plaza in Los Angeles) with the Pico House in the distance. The Plaza will be addressed in the Parks chapter of this book.

The Pico House is located at 410 N. Main Street in Plaza Park in downtown Los Angeles, north of the Hollywood Freeway (101), between Main Street and Alameda Street. Map Code: 634 G3.

GOODYEAR TIRE AND RUBBER PLANT (LOS ANGELES)

South of downtown Los Angeles, in the Florence District of the city, this is the site of lengthy scenes filmed for a 1927 Laurel and Hardy comedy classic.

« The Second Hundred Years »

Stan Laurel and Oliver Hardy are in prison in this, the 10th film the comedy team appeared in together. It is a landmark comedy film, as it was filmed in black-and-white with amber-tinted sequences.

The plot centers on Laurel and Hardy serving time in a large prison; their sole objective to escape. To accomplish this they dig a tunnel directly from their cell to the warden's office. After this "error," they are assigned to the dreaded task of breaking large rocks into small ones on a big rock pile that is supervised by a sneering prison guard (Stanley "Tiny" Sandford). Later a team of painters (not prisoners) who are working on the prison grounds leave for lunch. Seeing this, Laurel and Hardy turn their

BUILDINGS 45

The site of the 69th Street entrance to the Goodyear Tire and Rubber Plant, now a postal complex, the location of the prison gates seen in *The Second Hundred Years* (1927). (Photograph taken in 1998.)

prison uniforms inside out, grab paint brushes and buckets and easily walk from the prison grounds, passing through a large iron gate.

The "prison" seen in this 1927 film is the Goodyear Tire and Rubber Plant, located on Central Avenue, between Florence Avenue and Gage Avenue in South Central Los Angeles. The large iron gate convicts Laurel and Hardy passed through disguised as painters is the 69th Street entrance to the huge facility.

All buildings on this site were demolished years ago to make way for a post office complex.

This site is east of the Harbor Freeway (110). Map Code: 674 E7.

Car Lots

The Hal Roach Studios (Culver City)

Both new car dealerships and the dealers that exclusively sell used cars are located in virtually every neighborhood in the vast Los Angeles area.

It is well-known that the automobile is a necessity in Southern California, more so than in most areas across the nation because of the sudden dismantling of a transit system that crisscrossed the Los Angeles County area in the 1950s. A resurgence of a light rail surface transit system and an expanding subway system, however, will improve the public transportation crisis as time passes.

It was inevitable, then, that some car lots would be locations for motion pictures and television series.

THE HAL ROACH STUDIOS (CULVER CITY)

This location is a reverse location, so to speak, as a car dealership now rests on one of the most famous plots of land in motion picture history, the site of the Hal Roach Studios, where hundreds of comedies were produced for decades, including those of Harold Lloyd, Laurel and Hardy and Our Gang.

The small park east of the site of the Hal Roach Studios at the southwest corner of Washington Boulevard and National Boulevard. The marker commemorates the studio's contribution to the motion picture industry. (Photograph taken in 1984.)

The studios were founded by Hal Roach, who arrived in Los Angeles in 1913 and was fortunate enough to get acting parts in Western films at Universal Studios. Quickly tiring of that part of the industry and recognizing the potential of the fledgling industry, he delved into film production, which quickly led to the formation of the Hal Roach Studios which was in comedy film production as early as 1926.

During World War II, the studio complex was affectionately known as "Fort Roach" as a result of its involvement in the production of military training films, which were headed by a young actor turned Army officer, Ronald Reagan.

« Learn to Live »

Completed in February 1943, this is the first training film released by Fort Roach. Guy Kibbee stars as an angel complaining about too many U.S. pilots coming to heaven for not following established safety rules.

« Ditch and Live »

This 1943 training film stars Arthur Kennedy as a pilot who, with his crew, survives an airplane crash in the ocean.

« Land and Live in the Desert »

A 1943 instructional film showing airmen how to survive in the desert after an emergency landing.

« Resisting Enemy Interrogation »

Arthur Kennedy and Lloyd Nolan star as U.S. pilots, and Kent Smith is a German officer in this film relating the ordeal endured by prisoners of war undergoing kind and brutal interrogation by Germans after being captured.

This 1943 film was considered the most important produced at Fort Roach during World War II.

The advent of television in the 1950s seriously damaged the motion picture industry, resulting in the closing of many motion picture studios, including this one.

The entire complex was demolished and replaced by a large car dealership.

As a note of interest, a marker in a small park approximately 50 yards east of the site of the Hal Roach Studios claims to be the studio site.

The actual site of the complex is 8822 Washington Boulevard in Culver City.

This Culver City location is east of the San Diego Freeway (405) and south of the Santa Monica Freeway (10). Map Code: 632 H7.

Opposite: **The site of the Hal Roach Studios, 8822 W. Washington Boulevard, Culver City. (Photograph taken in 1990.)**

Caves

Bronson Canyon (Los Angeles)

BRONSON CANYON (LOS ANGELES)

Bronson Canyon, a remote canyon in the 4,500 acre Griffith Park complex on the edge of Hollywood, has two caves familiar to motion picture fans around the world as they have been locations in hundreds of movies for over 70 years.

The caves were originally the mines of a large rock quarry that supplied stone in the 1920s for a massive streetcar network that served the Los Angeles County area.

Segments of the following motion pictures, serials and television series productions were filmed, in part, at this location.

« Sagebrush Trail »

This 1933 motion picture features John Wayne in the typical cowboy saga prominent in the 1930s. The caves and canyon are prominent in the film, with one cave being an abandoned mine converted into an outlaw's hideout and the canyon being the location where Wayne is involved in an ambush and shootout near the end of the film.

« *The Vampire Bat* »

Obviously taking advantage of the horror film craze in the early 1930s, this 1933 motion picture suggests *Dracula* (1931) as it delves into blood-sucking bats. The plot centers on Lionel Atwill as the mad doctor in a small community searching for a blood substitute, a search that costs many their lives. *Dracula* cast member Dwight Frye runs through the caves chasing swarms of bats.

« *The Last Days of Pompeii* »

In this 1935 film Preston Foster stars as a blacksmith who later becomes a successful gladiator in the doomed Roman resort before, during and after the horrific and deadly eruption of Mt. Vesuvius in 79 A.D. that took approximately 16,000 lives and buried the city. During the film, Foster and Alan Hale herded horses in and out of the caves.

« *Dude Cowboy* »

Tim Holt portrays an agent of the Treasury Department who goes undercover on a dude ranch to bust a counterfeiting ring in this 1941 Western. The larger of the two caves is where the bad guys had their printing press hidden.

« *Sundown* »

The canyon is a part of North Africa in this 1941 film that relates the exploits of a native girl (Gene Tierney) who helps British troops in their efforts to defeat German forces during the early days of World War II.

« *The Lone Ranger* »

Clayton Moore and Jay Silverheels reprise their roles as the Lone Ranger and Tonto in this 1956 motion picture that has the immortal team of the Old West attempting to solve unrest between whites and Indians.

The trouble is brought on by a rich rancher (Lyle Bettger) who resists the efforts of the whites to have the territory become a state. The canyon is a remote part of the territory.

« *The Searchers* »

The canyon is prominent in this 1956 film that features John Wayne as a veteran of the Civil War who spends years in a seemingly hopeless search for a niece (Natalie Wood) who was kidnapped by the Indians.

« *V: The Final Battle* »

This 1984 television movie is the sequel to *V*, a 1983 release, and continues the saga of visitors from space who feign friendship and then attempt to establish a dictatorship on Earth.
The cave and the canyon are the location where the visitors held an exchange with earthlings, trading a hostage for a wanted man.

« *Sometimes They Come Back ... Again* »

In this 1996 sequel to the 1991 movie *Sometimes They Come Back*, the cave and the canyon are locations in a flashback sequence. The cave is the location outside the city of Glenrock where devil worshippers bring demons up from a deep pit to serve. Michael Gross stars.

« *The Lone Ranger Rides Again* »

Robert Livingston is the Lone Ranger in this 15 chapter 1939 serial, riding in and out of the canyon many times as he helps settlers who are continually harassed by an evil cattle baron. Tonto, the Lone Ranger's faithful Indian companion, is portrayed by Chief Thunder Cloud.

Opposite: **Bronson Canyon's famous caves, located on the west wall of the canyon. (Photograph taken in 1986.)**

A cave near the entrance to Bronson Canyon, the location of Batman's Bat Cave. (Photograph taken in 1986.)

« Superman »

Kirk Alyn portrays Superman/Clark Kent in this 15 chapter 1948 serial that has the "Man of Steel" dueling with the dangerous "Spider Lady" (Carol Forman) to save Metropolis from the effects of a deadly reducer ray.

The cave is first seen in chapter 2, as the entrance to the Spider Lady's hideout, which is reached by an elevator in chapter 4. In chapter 12, Superman uncovers the lair near "Question Crossing."

« The Adventures of Brisco County, Jr. » (1993-1994)

This critically acclaimed television series stars Bruce Campbell in the title role as a Harvard-educated man who came west in search of the men who killed his father. Even though this series is set in the Old West, it has a sci-fi flavor, as in chapter 1, "The Blast Supper," a group of Chinese workers find a mysterious ball-type object in a cave in Central California, near San Francisco. The cave shown is the larger of two in the canyon wall. The object, dubbed an "Unearthed Foreign Object" (UFO) or the "Mysterious Orb," is lost, found and lost throughout the series, the result of the efforts of Campbell and the ultimate bad guy, John Bly (Billy Drago).

The canyon is the location of a small oil well that provided oil for the motorcycles of a gang in a later chapter in the series.

« Emergency » (1972–1977)

Robert Fuller stars as Dr. Kelly Brackett, who is on the staff of a local hospital where Squad 51 of the Los Angeles County Fire Department brings those in need of emergency medical treatment. Randolph Mantooth and Kevin Tighe are the principal paramedics.

The canyon is the location of several emergencies Squad 51 rolled on in this television series.

« The Lone Ranger » (1949–1957)

As soon as the musical strains of Rossini's *William Tell Overture* begin, millions of fans immediately know that the Lone Ranger (Clayton Moore) and Tonto (Jay Silverheels) will ride across their television screens toward another adventure to bring law and order to the West.

Although the majority of location filming was done at the Iverson Ranch in the Chatsworth area of Los Angeles, many series segments were filmed in the canyon and at the two caves.

The Iverson Ranch will be addressed in the Ranches chapter of this book.

« Murder, She Wrote » (1984–1996)

This long-running television series is one of a very few wherein the lead character is a woman. Set far away from Hollywood, in Cabot Cove,

Maine, Jessica Fletcher (Angela Lansbury), a famous mystery writer, becomes involved in numerous murder investigations both in Cabot Cove and in cities across the United States and in other countries as she travels to promote her books.

The canyon is a New Mexico valley, the site of an archaeological dig for Indian artifacts in one episode.

« Wonder Woman » (1976–1979)

A comic book character created by Charles Moulton, Wonder Woman (Lynda Carter), a princess from remote Paradise Island who is endowed with super powers, comes to America during World War II to help fight the evil Germans.

The canyon and the caves are in several episodes of this television series.

As a note of interest, the solitary cave near the entrance to the canyon was used exclusively as the entrance to Batman's Bat Cave during the television series (1966–1968).

Bronson Canyon and the caves are located in Griffith Park, north of Franklin Avenue and the Hollywood Freeway (101) near the north end of Canyon Drive. Note: To reach the canyon, follow a narrow dirt road east from Canyon Drive for approximately one-fourth mile. Map Code: 593 G1.

Cemeteries

Forest Lawn Memorial Park–Glendale (Glendale)
Hollywood Memorial Park (Los Angeles)

Cemeteries in the greater Los Angeles area provide a final resting place for personalities connected with the entertainment industry as well as for persons from all walks of life.

As these serene locales honor the departed, motion picture and television series production companies generally do not film production segments on cemetery property. Occasionally, however, permission is gained, and film segments are completed as quickly and as quietly as possible.

The following cemeteries are not only motion picture and television series sites, but the location of the graves of motion picture personalities who appeared together in many film productions.

FOREST LAWN MEMORIAL PARK–GLENDALE (GLENDALE)

Forest Lawn Memorial Park–Glendale is the final resting place of many entertainment celebrities, including Jeanette MacDonald, who

58 CEMETERIES

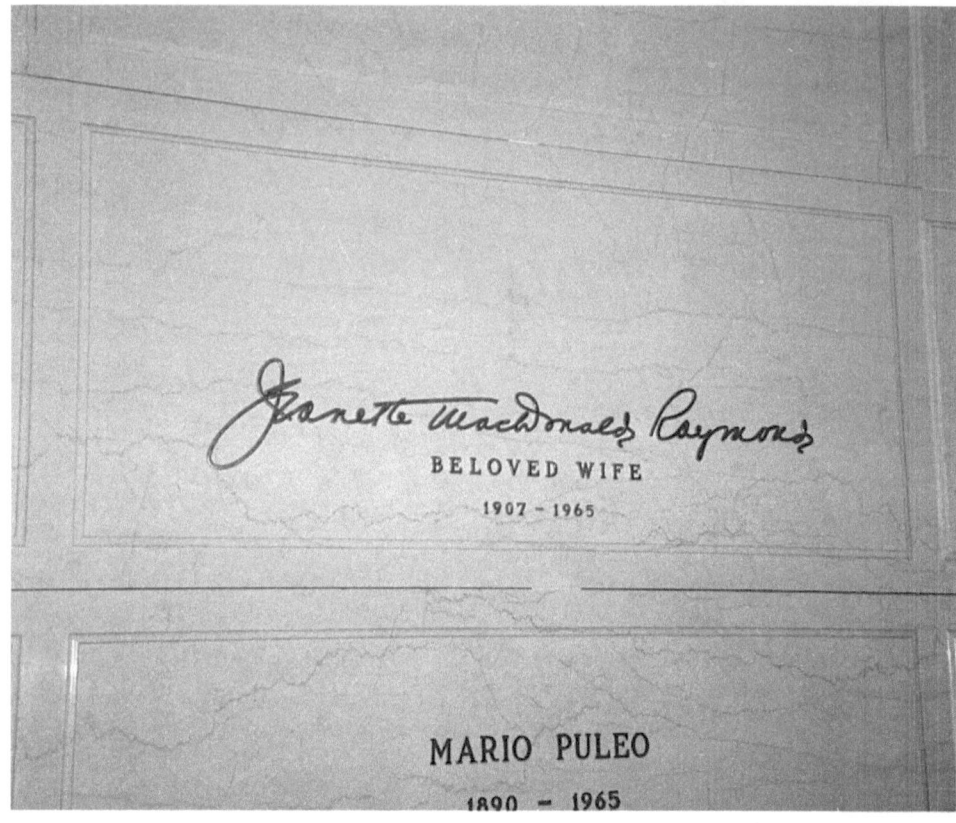

The Forest Lawn Memorial Park-Glendale Cemetery crypt of Jeanette MacDonald in the Freedom Mausoleum, Sanctuary of Heritage. (Photograph taken in 1995.)

starred with Nelson Eddy in eight classic musical motion pictures. Eddy is buried at Hollywood Memorial Park which is listed next in this chapter.

MacDonald is buried in Freedom Mausoleum, Sanctuary of Heritage; Humphrey Bogart, in the Garden of Memory, Eternal Light Section; Walt Disney, in Freedom Mausoleum, outside, left of entrance; Errol Flynn, in the Garden of Everlasting Peace; and Spencer Tracy, in the Garden of Everlasting Peace.

Forest Lawn Memorial Park–Glendale is located at 1712 Glendale Avenue, Glendale, California, north of the Glendale Freeway (2) and east of the Golden State Freeway (5). Map Code: 564 F7 and 594 F1 and G1.

HOLLYWOOD MEMORIAL PARK
(LOS ANGELES)

Hollywood Memorial Park, located so close to Hollywood, has more entertainment personalities resting there than any other cemetery in the United States.

Of special interest to the many *Our Gang* fans worldwide, both Carl "Alfalfa" Switzer and his girlfriend in the series, Darla Hood, rest here.

Switzer rests in Section 6, Lot 26, Grave 6; Hood, in Abbey of the Psalms, Crypt 7213, Corridor G-4; Cecil B. DeMille, in Section 8; Nelson

The Hollywood Memorial Park Cemetery gravesite of *Our Gang*'s Carl "Alfalfa" Switzer in Section 6, Lot 26, Grave 6. (Photograph taken in 1984.)

CEMETERIES 61

The Hollywood Memorial Park Cemetery crypt of *Our Gang*'s Darla Hood in the Abbey of the Psalms, Crypt 7213, Corridor G-4. (The upper left crypt in the photograph.) (Photograph taken in 1995.)

Eddy, in Section 8, Lot 89; Tyrone Power, in Section 8; and Rudolph Valentino, in Hollywood's Catholic Mausoleum, #1205, off Corridor A.

« *Virtuosity* »

The plot of this 1995 motion picture was previously addressed in the Auditoriums chapter.

Hollywood Memorial is the location Denzel Washington visits the gravesite of his wife and young daughter.

Opposite: The entrance to Hollywood Memorial Park Cemetery, 6000 Santa Monica Boulevard, Los Angeles. (Photograph taken in 1995.)

62 CEMETERIES

The Hollywood Memorial Park Cemetery gravesite of Nelson Eddy in Section 8, Lot 89. (Photograph taken in 1995.)

The following television series used this location regularly.

« *Unsolved Mysteries* » *(1988–1997)*

The plot of this television series will be addressed in the Churches chapter of this book.

This cemetery is a frequent location for a variety of segments throughout the series.

Hollywood Memorial Park is located at 6000 Santa Monica Boulevard in Los Angeles, south of the Hollywood Freeway (101). Map Code: 593 G6.

The Hollywood Memorial Park Cemetery crypt of Rudolph Valentino in Hollywood's Catholic Mausoleum, #1205, off Corridor A. (Photograph taken in 1995.)

Churches

St. Brendan's Church (Los Angeles)

Like all metropolitan areas across the United States, Los Angeles abounds in places of worship for all religions, ranging from small storefront churches to the magnificent Gothic structures dating back over 100 years.

It was inevitable that motion picture and television series production companies would use such buildings as locations, especially their exteriors.

ST. BRENDAN'S CHURCH (LOS ANGELES)

St. Brendan's Church, a typical Gothic-style structure of the 1920s, complete with magnificent spires, has proved to be a popular location for many motion picture and television series production companies, especially the Hal Roach Studios.

CHURCHES 65

St. Brendan's Church, 3rd Street and Van Ness Avenue in Los Angeles, a location in many films; most famous as a location in the closing scene of the 1953 sci-fi classic, *The War of the Worlds*. (Photograph taken in 1995.)

« Unsolved Mysteries » (1988–1997)

Robert Stack hosts this one-hour television series that focuses on unsolved murders, missing persons and assorted events of national interest, using interviews with persons associated with the cases and recreations of actual events.

St. Brendan's is a New York City church in a December 23, 1992, episode.

The church is located at the intersection of 3rd Street and Van Ness Avenue in Los Angeles, west of the Hollywood Freeway (101). Map Code: 633 G1.

City Halls

Beverly Hills City Hall (Beverly Hills)
Los Angeles City Hall (Los Angeles)

The majority of communities across the United States have city halls that serve as the centerpiece of civic activities and that house the offices of elected representatives.

The Southern California area has a variety of city halls as so many cities, large and small, make up the megalopolis that is Los Angeles County. Over the decades, these buildings have become favorite locations for motion picture and television series production companies.

The following city halls have been repeatedly used as locations.

BEVERLY HILLS CITY HALL (BEVERLY HILLS)

The Beverly Hills City Hall reflects the Spanish-style architecture that was extremely popular in the Southern California area in the early 1900s.

This building was used in segments of the following motion pictures and television series.

« Troop Beverly Hills »

Shelley Long portrays a very rich and very bored Beverly Hills socialite who becomes the leader of her daughter's "Wilderness Girls" troop during an energetic contest in the wild country outside of Beverly Hills. The city hall is prominent in several scenes throughout this 1989 motion picture.

« Twin Sisters »

Stephanie Kramer has a dual role as twins, one of which is a high-priced call girl stalked by a killer. Frederic Forrest is the police detective who attempts to save the endangered twin.

The city hall is the site where one twin receives an award for community service in this 1992 motion picture.

« Danielle Steele's "Star" »

This 1993 motion picture covers 15 years in the lives of a country girl (Jennie Garth), who suddenly becomes a show-business personality, and the man she loves (Craig Bierko), who is deeply involved in an unhappy relationship. The city hall is in one lengthy scene.

« Beverly Hills Cop III »

Again in Beverly Hills, a Detroit cop (Eddie Murphy) tackles a counterfeiting ring operating in an amusement park in this 1994 follow-up to the 1984 and 1987 motion pictures. The city hall is again a location where Murphy teams with local cops.

« Murder, She Wrote » (1984–1996)

The plot of this television series was addressed in the Caves chapter. In the "Petrified Forest" episode, Jessica Fletcher (Angela Lansbury)

comes to the police department at the city hall to question a murder suspect (Penny Fuller).

As a note of interest, the city hall was the location of the marriage of magazine publisher Helen Gurley (Brown) to Hollywood producer Paul Brown in 1959.

The Beverly Hills City Hall is located at 450 N. Crescent Drive in Beverly Hills, east of the San Diego Freeway (405). Map Code: 632 G1.

LOS ANGELES CITY HALL (LOS ANGELES)

The Los Angeles City Hall, constructed of limestone from France, marble from Tennessee and gray granite from California, opened in 1928. Its 452-foot tower proved to be a downtown landmark, visible for miles until the skyscraper era began in the 1960s. This building became recognizable worldwide in the 1950s as the emblem on Sgt. Joe Friday's badge #714, flashed in each opening and closing segment of the long-running *Dragnet* television series.

Because of the 1994 earthquake in Southern California that seriously damaged thousands of buildings in the Los Angeles area, this historic building is undergoing major repairs and retrofitting. The massive project began in 1998 and will continue for the next three-and-a-half years.

Segments of interior or exterior scenes of the following motion pictures and television series productions were filmed at this building.

« *While the City Sleeps* »

This 1928 film stars Lon Chaney as a tough detective solving mysteries and is the first motion picture filmed at the city hall as segments of it were filmed here shortly after construction of the building was completed and it opened for business.

Opposite: **The Beverly Hills City Hall, 450 N. Crescent Drive, Beverly Hills. (Photograph taken in 1995.)**

The author's father-in-law, George Mogelberg, at the Los Angeles City Hall, the location of several of his film appearances. (Photograph taken in the 1950s.)

« Outside the Wall »

Richard Basehart stars in this 1950 film about an ex-con who, attempting to go straight, helps put an end to a robbery syndicate.

The Main Street entrances of this building are locations in several scenes, one being a lengthy one wherein George Mogelberg makes one of several motion picture and television series appearances as a uniformed guard at his Main Street post.

« While the City Sleeps »

This 1956 remake of the 1928 film of the same title stars Dana Andrews and Ida Lupino as a policeman and a reporter attempting to stop a mad killer from killing again.

CITY HALLS 71

The Los Angeles City Hall's Spring Street (west) entrance, a location in scores of films. (Photograph taken in 1998.)

« Get Out of Town »

Douglas Wilson and Jeanne Baird star in this 1962 motion picture that focuses on the plight of an ex-gangster attempting to find the killer of his brother.

« Best Seller »

A police detective (Brian Dennehy) who is also a novelist is approached by a former hit man (James Woods) who wants Dennehy to write a novel based on his life of crime in this 1987 motion picture.
The city hall is the Police Evidence Depository Station in the opening segment of the film where Woods and two accomplices come to steal evidence critical to an upcoming case.

« The Naked Gun: From the Files of Police Squad »

Screwball Lt. Frank Drebin (Leslie Nielsen) is at it again in this 1988 motion picture based on the *Police Squad* (1982) television sitcom. This time, Drebin attempts to stop an assassination.

« Another 48 Hrs. »

Eddie Murphy and Nick Nolte reprise their roles in *48 Hrs.* (1982) as a convict (Murphy) and a cop (Nolte) loose in Los Angeles in this 1990 film.

« Another Midnight Run »

Christopher McDonald takes Robert DeNiro's 1988 *Midnight Run* role as a bounty hunter in this 1990 motion picture.

« Die Hard 2 »

Bruce Willis is once again in deep trouble in this 1990 sequel to *Die Hard* (1988).

« The Two Jakes »

In this 1990 sequel to *Chinatown* (1974), Jack Nicholson again stars as Jake Gittes, a private investigator involved in bad real-estate dealings in 1940s Los Angeles.

« Barton Fink »

In this 1991 movie, John Turturro stars as a screenwriter who comes to the professional insanity of 1941 Hollywood.

« Bugsy »

Warren Beatty stars as Benjamin "Bugsy" Siegel in this 1991 motion picture that focuses on Siegel's determined efforts to establish a casino in remote Las Vegas, Nevada, in the 1940s. The fabulous Flamingo Casino is the result of his determination.

« Ricochet »

Denzel Washington is an instant hero in this 1991 action-drama when he makes an outstanding arrest of a psycho (John Lithgow) who later plans to get revenge.

« White Hot: The Mysterious Murder of Thelma Todd »

The city hall is prominent in this 1991 television movie that goes back in time to a Los Angeles of the 1930s to delve into the short life and untimely death of movie star Thelma Todd (Loni Anderson).

« The Bodyguard »

In this 1992 film, an ex–Secret Service agent (Kevin Costner) is hired to protect a popular singer (Whitney Houston).

« Final Analysis »

The city hall is a San Francisco court building in this suspenseful 1992 movie starring Richard Gere as a psychiatrist who slowly becomes deeply involved with Kim Basinger, the sister of one of his patients.

« Hero »

In this 1992 movie, a man (Dustin Hoffman) saves the lives of many people shortly after an airplane crashes, but another man (Andy Garcia) takes all the credit.

« Bloodlines: Murder in the Family »

Elliott Gould, married to Mimi Rogers for 18 years, is suddenly charged with the murder of his parents in this 1993 motion picture. The Main Street side of the city hall is the entrance to a police station/prison.

« It's Nothing Personal »

The city hall is a police records division building in this 1993 motion picture starring Amanda Donohoe as a policewoman who quits the department and teams up with a bounty hunter to get a bail-jumper and avenge her brother.

« Shameful Secrets »

The city hall is a Maryland government building in this 1993 movie that stars Joanna Kerns as the battered wife of an extremely violent husband (Tim Matheson).

« Murder Between Friends »

Timothy Busfield stars in this 1994 motion picture about a grisly murder in New Orleans. The city hall is a New Orleans courthouse.

« One Woman's Courage »

The city hall is the Los Angeles County Courthouse in this 1994 movie starring Patty Duke as the witness of a murder who is stalked by the killer after a court acquittal.

« Speed »

In this 1994 action-drama, Keanu Reeves portrays a Los Angeles police officer who continually encounters a mad bomber (Dennis Hopper) determined to get millions of dollars by threatening the lives of innocent citizens of the city.

This building is the site of the annual Medal of Valor Awards given by the police department to those officers who have performed outstanding acts of courage.

Reeves receives this award for rescuing a group of persons in an elevator at a downtown high-rise building.

« Eraser »

A government agent (Arnold Schwarzenegger) does his best to hide and protect a woman from a bunch of bad guys in this 1996 action film.

« Eye for an Eye »

The plot of this 1996 motion picture was addressed in the Buildings chapter of this book.
The city hall is a court building where Sally Field sees the killer (Kiefer Sutherland) go free after the police and the justice system fail.

« For the Future: The Irvine Fertility Scandal »

The mishandling of embryos at a hospital is exposed by an employee in this 1996 motion picture starring Marilu Henner. The city hall is a Sacramento, California, state building.

« Mulholland Falls »

Nick Nolte stars as a lieutenant in the Los Angeles Police Department's famous "Hat Squad" of the 1950s in this 1996 movie whose plot centers on a woman who was murdered and who also was involved with Nolte and a U.S. Army general.
The city hall is a primary location in three scenes, the first being the downtown police station where the Hat Squad worked, the second being where Nolte first met an F.B.I. agent (Daniel Baldwin), and the final being the north Main Street entrance to the building where Nolte attacked Baldwin and tossed him from the building onto the sidewalk.

« A Thin Line Between Love and Hate »

Martin Lawrence, who also directed this 1996 film, stars as a man who boasts he can make love to a very hard-to-get woman. But the woman proves much harder to get rid of than she was to get.

The Los Angeles City Hall, 200 N. Spring Street, its image made famous on badge #714 of Sgt. Joe Friday in television's *Dragnet*. (Photograph taken in 1998.)

« Fathers' Day »

Two California men (Billy Crystal and Robin Williams) are suddenly told by a boy's mother (Natassja Kinski) that one is the father of her 16-year-old son who is a runaway, with the hope that one or both will find him and return him to her.

In this 1997 comedy, the Spring Street (west) entrance of this building is the location to enter a Los Angeles court building where Kinski first

confronts practicing lawyer Crystal with the news of her pregnancy some 17 years earlier.
This motion picture is a remake of the 1984 French film, *Les Compères.*

« *L.A. Confidential* »

Based on the novel by James Elroy, Los Angeles in the 1950s is the focus of this 1997 motion picture starring Kevin Spacey as a Los Angeles police sergeant, Kim Basinger as a hooker and Danny DeVito as a tabloid publisher looking for all the sleeze he can find in the community.
The city hall is in several scenes throughout this film.

« *Liar, Liar* »

Jim Carrey is at his comedic best in this 1997 uproarious movie centering on a man who told the truth and the many persons pleased and insulted by his remarks.

« *On the Line* »

The plot of this 1998 motion picture was previously addressed in the Buildings chapter of this book.
The city hall is the location of the offices of the district attorney where Linda Hamilton angrily confronts a deputy district attorney. Later in the film, the building is where Hamilton's peers from her squad room at the police station also confront the same deputy district attorney.

« *Beverly Hills 90210* » *(1990–   )*

This long-running series is the first in television history to have a zip code in its title. The series began with a family moving to Beverly Hills, California, from Minnesota and enrolling their 16-year-old twins (Jason Priestley and Shannen Doherty) in West Beverly High.

« Chicago Hope »
(1994–   )

This one-hour television medical drama stars Adam Arkin as surgeon Aaron Shutt and addresses the hectic activities at Chicago Hope Hospital.

« Kojak »
(1973–1978/1989–1990)

Lt. Theo Kojak (Telly Savalas) stars as a very aggressive New York City cop working out of the Manhattan South Precinct and solving countless major crimes over the years. The city hall is a New York City court and various other city government buildings throughout the television series.

« Land's End »
(1995–   )

Veteran police officer Mike Land (Fred Dryer) quits the department when the murderer of his wife goes free. Land moves to Cabo San Lucas in Baja, Mexico, becomes a private investigator, and teams with an old friend (Geoffrey Lewis). The city hall is a frequent location when Dryer is in Los Angeles in this television series.

« Players »
(1997–   )

In this television series, three parolees (Ice-T, Costas Mandylor and Frank John Hughes) work various assignments for the F.B.I., using their valuable expertise.

In the "Con Law" episode that aired nationally on October 24, 1997, the city hall is the location of a news conference held by a crooked attorney and the location where Ice-T met with an F.B.I. agent.

« *The Pretender* »
(1996–)

An organization, "The Centre," located and isolated a young pretender (a genius) in 1963 and exploited his genius for their lengthy research. As an adult, the genius, Jarod (Michael T. Weiss) escapes and dedicates his life to help those in need of help and to find justice for the wrongly accused. In doing so, Jarod assumes the roles of many persons.

« *The Rockford Files* »
(1974–1980)

Malibu, California, is the home (a trailer on the beach) of Jim Rockford (James Garner), a Los Angeles private investigator who served time in prison for a crime he didn't commit. During his many investigations for the rich and poor alike, Rockford gets to downtown Los Angeles often and into the city hall.

A two-hour made-for-television sequel to the series, *The Rockford Files: I Still Love L.A.*, was shown on CBS on November 27, 1994, and spawned a series of movies featuring Jim Rockford that continue to this day.

« *The Thorn Birds* »
(1983)

This 10-hour version of author Colleen McCullough's novel of the same title was the second-highest-rated miniseries ever televised at the time. Set in Australia, Richard Chamberlain stars as a Roman Catholic priest who must choose between the priesthood and the woman he loves (Rachel Ward).

« *The Trials of Rosie O'Neill* »
(1990–1992)

Cagney & Lacey costar Sharon Gless portrays Fiona "Rosie" O'Neill, a Beverly Hills attorney who leaves her practice to join the Los Angeles public defender's office. The city hall is a primary location throughout this television series.

« Unsolved Mysteries » (1988–1997)

This television series was addressed in the Churches chapter of this book. The city hall was a primary location in three episodes of the series. In 1992 it was the Cleveland, Ohio, City Hall where F.B.I. agent Eliot Ness was interviewed by the press relating to a series of murders in the 1930s that were later compared to the infamous 1947 Black Dahlia murder in Los Angeles. It can also be spotted in a 1993 segment relating to the assassination of Dr. Martin Luther King, Jr., and in a 1996 segment relating the details associated with the assassination of Robert F. Kennedy.

« Wild Palms » (1993)

This six-hour miniseries, set in Los Angeles in the year 2007, is a curious mix of film noir, science fiction and soap opera. Jim Belushi appears as Harry Wyckoff, a lawyer. His wife is played by Dana Delaney. The city hall is a city government building.

The Los Angeles City Hall is #150 in the city's Historic-Cultural Monuments listing.

The building is located at 200 N. Spring Street, south of the Hollywood Freeway (101) and east of the Harbor Freeway (110). Map Code: 634 G3.

Courts

Criminal Courts Building (Los Angeles)
Hall of Justice (Los Angeles)
Los Angeles County Municipal Courts Building (Los Angeles)
United States Government District Court Building (Los Angeles)

Traditionally, court buildings are located in the downtown area of the majority of communities across the United States, primarily for the convenience of the offices of district attorneys and city attorneys that are also traditionally located in the area and, of course, the civic center jails that hold prisoners awaiting hearings and trials.

The four major court buildings that serve the city of Los Angeles are conveniently located within sight of each other. They are the Criminal Courts Building, the Hall of Justice, the Los Angeles County Municipal Courts Building and the United States Government District Court Building.

Segments of the following motion pictures and television series were filmed in part in the interiors or the exteriors of these court buildings.

As major judicial entities, all four courts are not only well known in the city of Los Angeles, Southern California and throughout the United States, but in the majority of countries around the world, solely due to extensive local, national and worldwide news media coverage whenever celebrities in the entertainment industry and professional sports appear as defendants and witnesses in court preceedings.

CRIMINAL COURTS BUILDING (LOS ANGELES)

« The Case of the Hillside Stranglers »

Richard Crenna stars as Los Angeles police detective Bob Grogan, who was instrumental in apprehending Angelo Buono (Dennis Farina) and Kenneth Bianchi (Billy Zane), the infamous duo who murdered 10 women in 1977 and 1978 and dumped their bodies on Los Angeles hillsides.

This court building is the location of the offices of the Los Angeles County district attorney where Crenna discussed the ongoing case with a deputy district attorney in this 1989 motion picture.

The Criminal Courts Building's main entrance, 210 W. Temple Street in downtown Los Angeles. (Photograph taken in 1998.)

COURTS   83

The Criminal Courts Building's Spring Street jail van entrance where Orenthal James Simpson entered each court day during the 1995 murder trial. (Photograph taken in 1998.)

« Jury of One »

This 1992 motion picture centers on an intensive police investigation and search to locate a killer roaming city streets, from a story from the files of author Joseph Wambaugh. John Spenser of the *L.A. Law* television series stars. This building housed the offices of the district attorney in the film.

« Murder One »
(1995–   )

A rare television series wherein it is a continuing drama from a first degree murder case at the beginning of the season to the jury's verdict as the season concludes. Daniel Benzali portrayed lead defense attorney Teddy Hoffman during the debut season but was later replaced. This building is a primary location in the series.

84 COURTS

The building gained worldwide attention in 1975 due to the sensational Patty Hearst criminal trial after the kidnapped heiress, who participated in unlawful activities with a radical group, was captured and arrested. In 1995 it became the location of the Orenthal James Simpson double-murder trial that concluded with Simpson's acquittal.

The Criminal Courts Building is located at 210 W. Temple Street in downtown Los Angeles. Map Code: 634 G3.

HALL OF JUSTICE (LOS ANGELES)

This stately building with its distinctive columns that proudly served the citizens of Los Angeles City and Los Angeles County since the 1920s suffered great damage in the 1994 earthquake and is presently being demolished. But its many memories will live long in the minds of millions of citizens of the city, county and state.

Segments of the following motion pictures were filmed in part inside and outside of this building.

« The Indestructible Man »

The plot of this 1956 Lon Chaney, Jr., motion picture was addressed in the Buildings chapter.

In the film, this building is a police station where a detective relates a crime story to his peers.

« Dead-Bang »

A Los Angeles detective (Don Johnson) tracks a killer to hideouts in Colorado and Oklahoma in this 1989 action film.

The building is a police station where Johnson is assigned.

« The Distinguished Gentleman »

The Hall of Justice serves as a Washington, D.C., building in this 1992 motion picture that features Eddie Murphy as Florida con artist

The Spring Street entrance to the Hall of Justice (currently being demolished) in downtown Los Angeles. (Photograph taken in 1998.)

Thomas Jefferson Johnson who suddenly discovers the perks available in Congress far exceed those of his scams. He runs for office, is elected, and takes a seat in the House of Representatives.

« *Prophet of Evil: The Ervil LeBaron Story* »

Ervil LeBaron (Brian Dennehy), the leader of a small cult and a polygamist who is directly responsible for a series of murders from Mexico to the state of Utah in the 1970s, is pursued and brought to justice by a district attorney (William Devane) in this 1993 motion picture, based on actual incidents and police records.

The Hall of Justice is a Salt Lake City, Utah, court building, housing the offices of the county district attorney.

« Confessions: Two Faces of Evil »

Based on a true story, this 1994 motion picture centers on two men (Jason Batemen and James Wilder) who separately confess to the murder of a police officer.
The building is a court building in the film.

« Terror in the Family »

This 1996 motion picture focuses on domestic violence, but the abuser is an out-of-control teen (Hilary Swank), and Joanna Kerns is the abused mother.
The Hall of Justice is a court building in the film.
The North Broadway entrance to the building and the nearby northeast corner of Broadway and Temple Street attracted nationwide attention in 1970 when several women of the Manson family shaved their heads in protest of Charles Manson's being imprisoned in the building. The women sat on the sidewalk, attempting to make friends with anyone who would stop and listen, while making plans to assist Manson in an escape.
The Hall of Justice (soon to be a site) is located at 211 W. Temple Street in downtown Los Angeles. Map Code: 634 G3.

LOS ANGELES COUNTY MUNICIPAL COURTS BUILDING (LOS ANGELES)

Segments of the following motion pictures and television series were filmed, in part, at this building.

Opposite: **The northeast corner of Broadway and Temple Street with the Hall of Justice in the background, the location where members of the Manson family staged their sidewalk protest. (Photograph taken in 1998.)**

The Los Angeles County Municipal Courts Building's Grand Avenue entrance (110 N. Grand Avenue), a frequent film location in downtown Los Angeles. (Photograph taken in 1998.)

« The Case of the Hillside Stranglers »

The plot of this 1989 television movie was addressed earlier in this chapter.
This court building is the location where the preliminary hearing and subsequent trial were held for Angelo Buono (Dennis Farina).

« It's Nothing Personal »

As a courthouse, this building is the location of a lengthy trial for individuals suspected of committing robbery in this 1993 movie.

The Los Angeles County Municipal Courts Building's Hill Street entrance (the east side of the building), also a frequent film location. (Photograph taken in 1998.)

« Confessions: Two Faces of Evil »

This 1994 motion picture was previously addressed in this chapter. This building again served as a courthouse.

« Naked Gun 33⅓: The Final Insult »

This 1994 motion picture was previously addressed in the Auditoriums chapter of this book.
The building is a court building in the film.

« *Fast Company* »

The building is a court building in this 1995 movie.
The Los Angeles County Municipal Courts Building is located at 110 N. Grand Avenue in downtown Los Angeles. Map Code: 634 G3.

UNITED STATES GOVERNMENT DISTRICT COURT BUILDING (LOS ANGELES)

This building, also known as the Federal Building, houses federal judges and is where cases are heard in the federal judicial district encompassing the area in and surrounding Los Angeles.

Segments of the following motion pictures and television series productions were filmed inside or outside of this building.

« *Darkman* »

The plot of this motion picture will be addressed in the Tunnels chapter of this book.
This building is a federal court in several scenes in this 1990 film.

« *A House of Secrets and Lies* »

In this 1992 motion picture, Connie Sellecca portrays a very successful television newswoman who is consumed by suspicions, anger and guilt over a very unsuccessful marriage.
The building is a court building in the film.

Opposite: **The United States Government District Court Building, 312 N. Spring Street in downtown Los Angeles, a frequent film location. (Photograph taken in 1998.)**

« L.A. Law »
(1986–1994)

This television series was previously addressed in the Buildings chapter of this book.

This building is a location in two episodes of the series. First, it is a court building in a segment telecast on April 15, 1993, and later that year it is a criminal-civil court building in another episode.

The United States Government District Court Building is located at 312 N. Spring Street, east of the Pasadena Freeway (110) and south of the Hollywood Freeway (101), as are the other three court buildings listed in this chapter. Map Code: 634 G3.

Hospitals

Los Angeles County/USC Medical Center (Los Angeles)
Queen of Angels Hospital (Los Angeles)
Los Angeles Central Receiving Hospital (Los Angeles)

Hospital buildings and associated medical facilities provide locations, both interior and exterior, that would be difficult and extremely expensive for motion picture and television production companies to duplicate on studio back lots. Hospitals, then, both actively serving the public and those closed in the greater Los Angeles area, are regularly used to film motion picture and television series productions.

LOS ANGELES COUNTY/USC MEDICAL CENTER (LOS ANGELES)

Without question the most familiar hospital building in Los Angeles and around the world is the Los Angeles County/USC Medical Center (formerly Los Angeles County General Hospital) as, for many seasons, it appeared in the opening and closing shots of the popular television series, *General Hospital*.

A Los Angeles landmark for over seven decades, this huge medical complex has proven a popular location for motion picture and television series production companies.

The following motion pictures and television series were filmed, in part, at the hospital complex.

« *Hold Back the Dawn* »

In this 1941 motion picture, Charles Boyer, a European gigolo who is desperate to get into the United States from Mexico, meets and marries a vacationing schoolteacher (Olivia de Havilland), but things do not go as easily as Boyer planned.

The main building of the hospital complex is a primary location near the end of the film as Boyer, on the run from the police, visits an ill de Havilland in one of the hospital rooms.

« *The Case of the Hillside Stranglers* »

The plot of this 1989 television movie was previously addressed in the Courts chapter of this book.

This hospital is the site of a clinic where Kenneth Bianchi (Billy Zane), posing as a psychologist and using forged credentials, actually talked with patients.

« *Vital Signs* »

Jimmy Smits stars as the head surgeon of a large metropolitan hospital who guides a group of third-year medical students toward internship.

This hospital is the location of many interior scenes and the location of all exterior scenes in this 1990 motion picture.

« *The Rockford Files: Friends and Foul Play* »

This building is a primary location in this 1996 television movie featuring James Garner as Jim Rockford, a Los Angeles private investigator

The Los Angeles County/USC Medical Center, 1200 N. State Street in East Los Angeles, a frequent film location, most notable in television's *General Hospital*. (Photograph taken in 1998.)

who is digging into the events surrounding the murder of a waitress who was stalking the mobster she suspected of murdering her son.

« *Murder, She Wrote (1984–1996)* »

This television series was previously addressed in the Caves chapter of this book.

This building is the "Cabot Cove Emergency Hospital" in the "Final Curtain" episode in the series that aired on January 10, 1993.

As a note of interest, Busby Berkeley, the legendary genius of motion picture musicals in the 1930s and 1940s and a film director in the 1950s, was confined in this hospital's psychiatric ward in the 1940s after he attempted to take his own life.

The Los Angeles County/USC Medical Center complex is located at 1200 N. State Street, north of the San Bernardino Freeway (10) and east of the Golden State Freeway (5) in East Los Angeles. Map Code: 635 A3 & B3.

QUEEN OF ANGELS HOSPITAL (LOS ANGELES)

The Queen of Angels Hospital, a Hollywood landmark for decades and a frequently used shooting location, is presently owned by the Los Angeles International Church and is being renovated to serve church functions.

The following motion pictures and television series were filmed, in part, at this building.

« Men Don't Tell »

In a stark turnaround, a husband (Peter Strauss) is the victim of spousal abuse by an extremely jealous wife (Judith Light) in this 1993 motion picture.

Strauss is hospitalized with a series of injuries in this building near the end of the film.

« Snapdragon »

Steven Bauer and Pamela Anderson star in this 1993 motion picture relating the horrid tale of an amnesiac (Anderson) who is haunted by dreams of murder.

This building is a primary location in a lengthy scene in the film.

Opposite: The Queen of Angels Hospital, on Bellevue Avenue, between Coronado and Waterloo streets. (Photograph taken in 1998.)

« The Innocent »

This building is St. Ann's Hospital in this 1994 motion picture starring Kelsey Grammer, Dean Stockwell and Polly Draper in a story revolving around a child's witness of a murder and a cop's effort to save the boy from two killers who want to eliminate the only witness.

« The Invaders »

The plot of this 1995 motion picture was previously addressed in the Bridges chapter.
This hospital is the "U.S.C. Medical Center" in one lengthy scene.
The Queen of Angels Hospital complex is located on Bellevue Avenue, between Coronado Street and Waterloo Street, north of the Hollywood Freeway (101). Map Code: 634 D1.

LOS ANGELES CENTRAL RECEIVING HOSPITAL (LOS ANGELES)

The Los Angeles Central Receiving Hospital is included in this chapter for its historical importance to the community, nation and the world.
When the hospital opened on June 7, 1957, it replaced Georgia Street Receiving Hospital, which had been in operation for over 20 years. It proved to be the busiest emergency hospital in downtown Los Angeles for many years but nearly closed in 1969. It was saved when it was converted to a clinic in 1971 and is still operational.
This hospital made worldwide headlines in 1968 when Senator Robert F. Kennedy was brought to it shortly after he was shot at the Ambassador Hotel. He was later taken to the nearby Good Samaritan Hospital where he died.
The Los Angeles Central Receiving Hospital is located at 1401 W. 6th Street, south of the Hollywood Freeway (101). Map Code: 634 D3.

HOSPITALS 99

The south emergency entrance to the Los Angeles Central Receiving Hospital at 1401 S. 6th Street in Los Angeles, where a mortally wounded Robert F. Kennedy was brought from the Ambassador Hotel in 1968. (Photograph taken in 1998.)

Hotels

Biltmore Hotel (Los Angeles)
Queen Mary (Long Beach)

Hotels of varying sizes and styles exist in virtually every locale of the greater Los Angeles area and have been and continue to be used by motion picture and television series production companies for location filming.

The ages of these structures also vary, from the early to the late twentieth century.

The following hotels were used as primary locations in segments from the below listed motion pictures and television series.

BILTMORE HOTEL (LOS ANGELES)

Once a part of the original four-square leagues owned by the Pueblo of Los Angeles, the land is now the location of the magnificent Biltmore Hotel that opened on October 1, 1923. It quickly became a downtown Los Angeles landmark and over the years has attracted motion picture and television series production companies for interior and exterior location filming.

Segments of the following motion pictures and television series were filmed at this hotel.

The Biltmore Hotel, located at 506 S. Grand Avenue in downtown Los Angeles, facing Pershing Square Park. (Photograph taken in 1998.)

« *The Fat Man* »

Writer Dashiell Hammett's overweight detective (J. Scott Smart) investigates the death of a dentist, a case which eventually leads him to a showdown at a circus.

The hotel is a primary location early in this 1951 film.

« Vertigo »

One of director Alfred Hitchcock's best efforts, this 1955 film features James Stewart as a retired police detective who is hired in San Francisco to track the wife (Kim Novak) of a friend.

The hotel is noted for the 11 flights of wrought-iron stairs of the fire escape prominent in a dream-like sequence in the film.

« Dynasty: The Reunion »

Most of the cast from the "Dynasty" television series (1981–1989) get together two years later for a big reunion in this 1991 television movie.

The hotel is one of many seen in the film.

« Jack Reed: Badge of Honor »

This fact-based 1993 motion picture has Jack Reed (Brian Dennehy), a deputy sheriff, on the trail of a murder suspect (William Sadler) who is working undercover for the FBI.

The hotel is a primary location in the film.

« Jericho Fever »

The Biltmore is a Denver, Colorado, hotel in this 1993 motion picture that features Stephanie Zimbalist and Perry King attempting to track down a group of terrorists who unknowingly brought a deadly virus from Mexico to the United States.

« The Invaders »

This 1995 motion picture was previously addressed in the Bridges chapter.

The hotel is a location in one lengthy scene in the film.

« Evening Shade » (1990–1994)

This television sitcom was the first network series set in the state of Arkansas. Burt Reynolds stars as Wood Newton, the coach of the town of Evening Shade's high school football team. Marilu Henner appears as Wood's wife.

The Biltmore is a New York City hotel where Reynolds stays when brought to the Big Apple to appear on a television show with Terry Bradshaw and Bryant Gumble.

The Biltmore Hotel is located at 506 S. Grand Avenue in downtown Los Angeles, east of the Harbor Freeway (110). Note: If the (110) designation for both the Harbor Freeway and the Pasadena Freeway seems a bit confusing, the Pasadena Freeway is the northern extension of the Harbor Freeway. Map Code: 634 E4.

The hotel is #60 in the city's Historic-Cultural Monuments listing.

QUEEN MARY (LONG BEACH)

A most unusual hotel, the *Queen Mary*, now permanently docked 22 miles south of Los Angeles in the city of Long Beach, is a regular location for motion picture and television series production companies.

The 1,019-feet luxury liner was commissioned by Britain in 1935 and took its maiden voyage in 1936 under the Cunard Lines banner. After 101 trans–Atlantic crossings it was brought to the city of Long Beach, refurbished and opened to the public in 1971 as a 365-room floating hotel.

Segments of the following motion pictures and television series were filmed either in the ship's interior or on its decks, both when it was in service as an ocean liner and after its retirement.

« Dodsworth »

Author Sinclair Lewis' novel is brought to the screen in this 1936 motion picture. Walter Huston recreates his Broadway role as a wealthy married American businessman who retires and travels to Europe to find true love.

The ship is the location for Atlantic Ocean crossing scenes.

« Foreign Correspondent »

Joel McCrea stars as an American reporter sent to Europe to cover the events that began World War II in this 1940 motion picture. Film critics claim this to be director Alfred Hitchcock's masterpiece.
The ship is a location near the end of the film.

« Meet Danny Wilson »

Frank Sinatra is at his best, belting out old favorites in this 1952 motion picture about a young singer who signs a contract with a nightclub owner (Raymond Burr) who is also a crook.

« Mame »

Lucille Ball, in her final feature film, and Robert Preston star in this 1974 motion picture based on Jerry Herman's Broadway hit musical *Mame*, relating the years a young boy spent with his eccentric aunt (Ball).

« Farewell, My Lovely »

Robert Mitchum stars as private investigator Philip Marlowe in this 1975 motion picture. This third film version of the Raymond Chandler novel has Mitchum hot on the trail of a killer.

« W.C. Fields and Me »

A 1976 motion picture based on a novel by Carlotta Monti, the film relates the long-time relationship between Monti and the great comedian W.C. Fields, Rod Steiger stars as Fields and Valerie Perrine appears as Monti.
Lots of authentic Hollywood locations, including this ship.

The *Queen Mary*, a 1935 luxury liner, is now a 365-room hotel in Long Beach, California. (Photograph taken in 1988.)

« A Love Affair: The Eleanor and Lou Gehrig Story »

Blythe Danner and Edward Herrmann star in this 1978 movie as the wife and the baseball legend who was cut down in his prime by a deadly disease that bears his name.

« The Winds of War »

Author Herman Wouk adapted his novel for this 1983 television motion picture (series) that covers World War II from the early years to

The port (left) deck of the *Queen Mary*, a frequent film location. (Photograph taken in 1988.)

the Japanese sneak attack on Pearl Harbor, Hawaii, on December 7, 1941. Robert Mitchum stars as Victor "Pug" Henry, an American naval officer.

« *The Natural* »

Robert Redford and Robert Duvall star in this 1984 film adaptation of Bernard Malamud's novel about a young man (Redford) who has an exceptional ability to play baseball.

« *Treacherous Crossing* »

Lindsay Wagner stars in this 1992 movie that centers on the disappearance of the husband of a wealthy woman on their honeymoon cruise on the *Queen Mary*.

« Batman Forever »

The Caped Crusader (Val Kilmer) finally teams with Robin (Chris O'Donnell) in this 1995 action-adventure. The heroes battle Two-Face (Tommy Lee Jones) and the Riddler (Jim Carrey) to save the citizens of Gotham City.

« The Elizabeth Taylor Story »

A biography of the legendary screen star, this 1995 biographical movie stars Sherilyn Fenn as Taylor and an assortment of actors portraying her many husbands: Michael Wilding (Nigel Havers), Eddie Fisher (Corey Parker), Mike Todd (Ray Wise) and William McNamara as Montgomery Clift, the actor reported to be Taylor's first love.

This ship is a primary location in a lengthy scene wherein Taylor returns to the United States from Europe.

« Cable Guy »

In this 1996 black comedy, Jim Carrey takes the role of a cable television installer who forces his friendship on a customer (Matthew Broderick), a man who simply wants solitude.

« Batman and Robin »

This 1997 motion picture has George Clooney as the Caped Crusader and Chris O'Donnell returning as Robin. Bat Girl (Alicia Silverstone) finally appears, and the trio go into the streets of Gotham City to rid the community of evil.

« Out to Sea »

In their eighth film appearance together in 31 years, veteran actors Jack Lemmon and Walter Matthau portray brothers-in-law who are hired by a cruise line to be escorts for lonely rich women and teach them how to dance. The only problem is that Lemmon and Matthau, both in this 1997 comedy and in real life, are horrible dancers. Dyan Cannon and Gloria DeHaven also star.

This ship is a primary location for many scenes in the film.

« *Beverly Hills 90210* » *(1990–)*

This television series was previously addressed in the City Halls chapter.

This ship is a location in the 1996 season-ending episode.

Beginning in 1973 and continuing to date, minor segments for episodes of the following television series were filmed on the *Queen Mary*:

Airwolf (1984–1988)
Baywatch (1989–)
The Bionic Woman (1976–1978)
B.J. and the Bear (1979–1981)
Blue Thunder (1984)
The Bold and the Beautiful (1987–)
Cannon (1971–1976)
Charlie's Angels (1976–1981)
CHiPs (1977–1983)
Ferris Bueller (1990-1991)
The Hardy Boys/Nancy Drew Mysteries (1977–1979)
Harry O (1974–1976)
MacGyver (1985–1992)
Murder, She Wrote (1984–1996)
The Night Stalker (1974-1975)
Police Woman (1974–1978)
Quantum Leap (1989–1993)
Quincy, M.E. (1976–1983)
The Rookies (1972–1976)
seaQuest DSV (1993–1995)
Sightings (1992–)
Switch (1975-1976)
Toma (1973-1974)
Unsolved Mysteries (1988–1997)
The Young and the Restless (1973–)

Lakes

Arboretum of Los Angeles County (Arcadia)
Toluca Lake (Burbank)

The greater Los Angeles area has many lakes, primarily situated in parks that provide year-around enjoyment for citizens of the communities.

Many lakes have been the location for motion picture and television series segments over the years and continue to be used for that purpose.

The following were primary locations for film segments of the below listed motion pictures.

ARBORETUM OF LOS ANGELES COUNTY (ARCADIA)

The Arboretum of Los Angeles County is a 127-acre complex located in Arcadia, California, north of the city of Los Angeles. Within this acreage, near the south end of the complex, is a large lake that is listed as a lagoon in arboretum literature. Many refer to this lake as the *Fantasy Island* lagoon as it was seen in the opening segments of each episode of this television series wherein a small seaplane lands in it bringing guests to the island to live out a fantasy.

Since 1937, over 100 motion pictures and scores of television specials, series productions and mini-series have been filmed at this location.

The California Arboretum Foundation printed a booklet listing these film productions from 1937 to its last printing in 1984. Because of budget restraints, an updated version of the booklet has been delayed, and it is uncertain when the new version will be available.

Virtually all 127 acres have been utilized for a variety of film segments; the following filmed in and near the lagoon and the adjoining jungle area.

« *The Letter* »

A remake of the 1940 motion picture that starred Bette Davis, this 1982 release has Lee Remick in the lead as a murderess who attempts to escape punishment by pleading self-defense. Several scenes were filmed at the lagoon.

« *Stick* »

The lagoon's dock is a location in this 1985 motion picture starring Burt Reynolds as an ex-con who gets involved with drug smugglers as he attempts to avenge the death of a friend.

« *P.O.W. the Escape* »

David Carradine stars as one of a group of American P.O.W.s who fight their way through the jungle to freedom as Saigon falls in the Vietnamese conflict in this 1986 action-drama. Many scenes were filmed in and near the lagoon.

« *Unnatural Causes* »

In this 1986 drama, Alfre Woodard and John Ritter star as a Veterans Administration counselor and a Vietnam veteran struggling to prove that Agent Orange caused an illness. The jungle area served as a Vietnamese jungle.

« Who's That Girl? »

Madonna attempts comedy in this 1987 film, portraying a recently released prisoner being escorted out of town. The jungle area is a location in one lengthy scene.

« Three Fugitives »

Nick Nolte and Martin Short star as a clumsy bank robber and a hostage who was just released from prison in this 1989 comedy. The lagoon is a location in several scenes.

« The Forbidden Dance »

Former Miss U.S.A. Laura Herring portrays a jungle princess who comes to America from Brazil in an effort to save endangered rain forests. The jungle area serves as a section of a Brazilian rain forest in this 1990 film.

« Lord of the Flies »

This 1990 remake of the 1963 British motion picture has American kids stranded in a remote area. The jungle is a primary location throughout the film.

« Meet the Applegates »

Stockard Channing and Dabney Coleman star in this 1991 comedy whose plot centers on Brazilian beetles (in human form) who come to the United States to obtain their quota of human prey. The lagoon is a part of the Amazon River in lengthy scenes.

« Terminator 2: Judgment Day »

A cyborg from the future (Arnold Schwarzenegger) comes to the present to protect a soon-to-be-great man from destruction by a rival

terminator in this 1991 action-adventure. The jungle is a location in several scenes.

« *Dave* »

The production company constructed a facade of the White House near the lagoon for many scenes in this 1993 motion picture that stars Kevin Kline as a look-alike who replaces the president when the president is incapacitated by a stroke.

« *The American President* »

Michael Douglas portrays a widowed U.S. president who falls for a lobbyist (Annette Bening) in this 1995 romantic comedy. Several scenes were shot near the lagoon.

« *The Phantom* »

The masked, purple-clad hero (Billy Zane) who first appeared in the February 1938 issue of Ace Comics (in a brown costume) and on screen in a 15-chapter serial in 1943, finally appears in a motion picture in this 1996 release, preventing bad guys from stealing a group of mystical skulls that have legendary powers which are hidden in a dense jungle.

Several scenes were filmed in the jungle area and around the lagoon.

« *Spy Hard* »

A James Bond spoof, this 1996 motion picture stars Leslie Nielsen as Agent WD-40, who is hot on the trail of master criminal General Rancor (Andy Griffith). Several scenes were filmed at the lagoon.

The Arboretum of Los Angeles County's lagoon and a portion of the jungle area, both very frequently used film locations. (Photograph taken in 1986.)

« *Anaconda* »

Jennifer Lopez stars in this 1997 motion picture about a snake hunter and a film crew who venture into the jungle and encounter a monster boa. A fake waterfall was constructed at the lagoon, and several boa encounters were filmed.

The lagoon is also known as "Tarzan's Lagoon" because so many Tarzan motion pictures were filmed there and at the nearby "Prehistoric and Jungle Garden" that borders the north side of the lake.

The lake was a primary location for the following Tarzan motion pictures.

« *Tarzan and the Slave Girl* »

In this 1950 motion picture, the 19th Tarzan movie, Lex Barker takes the role of Tarzan and Vanessa Brown is Jane in a jungle tale that pits the Ape Man against a tribe of lion worshippers.

« *Tarzan's Peril* »

Lex Barker is back as Tarzan in this 1951 motion picture, the 20th on Tarzan, this time outwitting gun-runners who are stirring up a lot of trouble between warring tribes. Virginia Huston appears as Jane.

« *Tarzan's Hidden Jungle* »

Gordon Scott debuts as Tarzan in this 1955 entry, the 23rd in the series of Tarzan motion pictures filmed, and matches wits with a hunter (Jack Elam) who is randomly killing jungle animals, just for the fun of it.

This film is notable as it proved to be the last Tarzan motion picture to be shot at this location.

The Arboretum of Los Angeles County is located at 301 N. Baldwin Avenue, south of the Foothill Freeway (210) in Arcadia, California. Map Code: 567 A5.

Toluca Lake (Burbank)

Toluca Lake is partially situated in the Toluca Lake District of Los Angeles and in the southwest corner of Burbank, immediately north of Universal Studios and west of the Warner Brothers Studios, and adjoins the Lakeside Country Club, part of which is the Lakeside Golf Club of Hollywood where many Hollywood entertainment personalities played golf in the golden days of Hollywood and continue to do so today.

The following Hal Roach Our Gang comedy was filmed, in part, at this location.

Toluca Lake, 4500 Lakewide Drive, Burbank, California. (Photograph taken in 1995.)

« Three Men in a Tub »

The 164th entry in the Our Gang series and their 75th talkie, this 1938 film features the Gang in a boat race for the "Championship of Toluca Lake," a race prompted by Alfalfa's (Carl Switzer) jealousy over Darla's (Darla Hood) attention to rival Waldo (Darwood Kaye) and Waldo's boat, a sleek speedboat that zips the two up and down the lake.

To compete, Alfalfa and Spanky (George McFarland) and some of the Gang construct a boat out of neighborhood junk, and the race is on in the calm waters of Toluca Lake.

The Lakeside Country Club and Toluca Lake are located at 4500 Lakeside Drive in Burbank, California, south of the Ventura Freeway (134) and north of the Hollywood Freeway (101). Map Code: 563 D5.

Mansions

Arden Villa (Pasadena)
Greystone Mansion (Beverly Hills)

The next step up from a very upscale house, a mansion is considered an expensive abode, generally priced in the million-dollar-and-up range in the greater Los Angeles area.

Mansions, however, are not concentrated in one particular part of the city or county although Beverly Hills has its share. Generally speaking, they are sprinkled from the Pacific Ocean far eastward to the magnificent hills of Simi Valley and beyond.

The following mansions are primary locations for various scenes in the below listed motion pictures and television series productions.

ARDEN VILLA (PASADENA)

The Arden Villa is a 20,000-square-foot mansion located in the heart of the upscale residential area of the city of Pasadena, California. Even though many segments of motion pictures and television series have been filmed at this location, it is a private residence and can't be entered without the permission of the owner.

« Cops »

Several sight gags keep Buster Keaton one big step in front of hundreds of policemen in this 1922 silent comedy, the 28th in Buster Keaton's lengthy career and a film many critics and fans believe to be his best effort.

The mansion's front gate is the location of the entryway into the home of Buster Keaton's sweetheart (Virginia Fox), a rich girl who continually rejects him because he is a failure at every business venture he enters.

« Duck Soup »

This 1933 motion picture stars the immortal comedy team, the Marx Brothers (Groucho, Chico, Harpo and Zeppo).

The four are in the tiny nation of Freedonia, where Groucho, brought to the nation as a dictator to stop the threats of neighboring Sylvania, causes, as usual, continual confusion to a final but pleasing conclusion.

This mansion's large patio is the location of a garden party held to welcome Groucho to Freedonia.

« St. Ives »

In this 1976 movie, Charles Bronson is cast as a struggling writer who becomes involved with a wealthy man (John Houseman) and beautiful Jacqueline Bisset in a murder.

The gated entrance to the mansion is a location seen several times throughout the film.

« Dynasty »
(1981–1989)

A popular prime-time television series similar to *Dallas*, this popular show focuses on a wealthy family residing in Denver, Colorado, with all of the family problems one family could have, and then more.

The gated entrance to the Arden Villa, 1145 Arden Road, Pasadena, California, a frequent film location. (Photograph taken in 1988.)

John Forsythe stars as Blake Carrington, the head of the clan. Linda Evans is divorcée Krystle Jennings, who marries Blake. Joan Collins, who came along in later episodes, is Blake's ex-wife, Alexis Carrington.

The Carringtons' mansion was, at times, this mansion with the fictional address of 173 Essex Drive in Denver.

Undoubtedly, the most remembered scene filmed at the mansion is the catfight between Evans and Collins that ends up in a pond adjacent to the mansion's patio.

The Arden Villa is located at 1145 Arden Road, east of Lake Avenue and south of the Foothill Freeway (210) in Pasadena, California. Map Code: 566 B6.

Greystone Mansion (Beverly Hills)

Beverly Hills, California, is the appropriate location for the Greystone Mansion, the spacious and architecturally beautiful former home of the wealthy Doheny family. This sprawling estate and its lovely gardens are open to the public and are a favorite location for motion picture and television series production companies.

The following motion picture and television series were filmed, in part, in the mansion and on the mansion grounds.

As a note of interest, the arched entrance and the adjoining courtyard are most often seen in production segments as the entrance to the mansion. Actually, this arch serves as the rear entrance.

« Flowers in the Attic »

Victoria Tennant and Louise Fletcher star in this 1987 motion picture that relates the horrors suffered by siblings who are imprisoned in a mansion by their psychotic mother and grandmother.

« The Inheritance »

This 1997 television movie stars Meredith Baxter as Beatrice and Tom Conti as her husband, Henry. The wealthy couple reside at the beautiful Evenswood Mansion. Cari Shayne portrays Edith, a servant at the mansion who eventually inherits it, and Thomas Gibson stars as James, Edith's romantic interest and eventual husband.

The movie is based on author Louisa May Alcott's first novel.

Greystone is, of course, Evenswood Mansion, seen in the distance as coaches approach, and from a family graveyard.

The mansion's courtyard is where family and guests arrived; the mansion's side yard and fountain, where they played archery games.

The mansion's garage area serves as a stable area in this film.

Opposite: **The spacious Greystone Mansion, situated at 905 Loma Vista Drive, Beverly Hills, California. (Photograph taken in 1986.)**

The Greystone Mansion's garage area, often used as a garage and a stable in film productions. (Photograph taken in 1986.)

« Dynasty: The Reunion »

The plot of this 1991 television movie was previously addressed in the Hotels chapter.
Greystone is a mansion owned by a wealthy family in this film.

« Murder, She Wrote »
(1984–1996)

The plot of this television series was previously addressed in the Caves chapter of this book.
This mansion is used often during the long run of this series.
In a 1985 episode, "Reflections of the Mind," the mansion is said to be in Cincinnati, Ohio.

In a 1990 episode, "One White Rose for Death," Greystone is the British Embassy in Washington, D.C.

In a 1991 episode, the mansion is said to be in Louisville, Kentucky.

In the 1994 season premier episode that aired nationally on September 25, Jessica Fletcher (Angela Lansbury) travels to several locations, including the mansion, to investigate a murder.

The Greystone Mansion is located at 905 Loma Vista Drive, north of Sunset Boulevard and east of the San Diego Freeway (405) in Beverly Hills, California. Map Code: 592 F5.

The mansion that never existed is mentioned at this point simply because it is an integral part of the plot of a classic Hal Roach film.

« *Small Talk* »

The 89th Our Gang film, released in 1929, is the first of the Gang's talking pictures.

While in the "mansion," Gang member Wheezer's (Bobby Hutchins) new home, cute Jean Darling accidentally sets off the fire/police alarm, which results in the immediate response of police and fire vehicles rushing toward the mansion, turning from Culver Boulevard in Culver City onto Lafayette Place, and skidding to a stop at the curb across the street from a row of houses.

The houses at this location are "normal" houses of typical 1920s California architecture and were not used as locations in this film.

The mansion (interiors) seen throughout the second half of this film were all located on the back lot of the Hal Roach Studios.

Movie Studios

Charlie Chaplin Studio (Hollywood)
Columbia Pictures Entertainment Studios (Culver City)
Metro-Goldwyn-Mayer Studios (Culver City)
Paramount Studios (Hollywood)
Hal Roach Studios (Culver City)
Sennett Studios (Los Angeles)
20th Century–Fox Studios (Los Angeles)
Universal Pictures Studios (Universal City)

Los Angeles and Culver City boasted the majority of the world's major motion picture studios from the 1920s through the 1950s. Several of these studios have faded into motion picture history, but some remain, still producing films for worldwide distribution.

It would be impossible to list all films produced at the ten studios to be addressed in this chapter. Instead, I will list motion pictures these studios are famous for or motion pictures of importance shot at a location in close proximity to the studio or studio property.

Opposite: The former Charlie Chaplin Studio, 1416 N. La Brea Avenue, Hollywood, California. (Photograph taken in 1988.)

CHARLIE CHAPLIN STUDIO (HOLLYWOOD)

One of the few film studio buildings remaining in Hollywood, the Charlie Chaplin Studio was billed as the first complete motion picture studio in Hollywood when it opened in 1919. Owned by the legendary comedian of silent films, Charlie Chaplin, the studio churned out hundreds of Chaplin short comedies and feature films. Aside from a slight reduction in size from its 1919 acreage, the studio buildings appear the same today as they did over eight decades ago.

« Chaplin »

The golden age of Hollywood is recreated for this 1992 film tribute to the life of Charlie Chaplin, making it fitting that this studio is a primary location in many scenes in the film.

Chaplin's life is traced from London, England, poverty to his arrival in Hollywood and his association with film director Mack Sennett, then to international stardom and finally into a sex scandal that eventually leads to his self-imposed exile in Europe.

The Charlie Chaplin Studio property is now occupied by A&M Records, a company founded by the former owners, Herb Alpert and Jerry Moss.

The studio is #58 in the city's Historic-Cultural Monuments listing and is located at 1416 N. La Brea Avenue, south of Hollywood Boulevard and south of the Hollywood Freeway (101) in Hollywood. Map Code: 593 D5.

COLUMBIA PICTURES ENTERTAINMENT STUDIOS (CULVER CITY)

The administration building of Columbia Pictures Entertainment Studios (Culver Studios), completed in 1919, was originally the headquarters of the Thomas H. Ince Studios, which produced and released hundreds of silent motion pictures. The studio changed owners often during the years of talking motion pictures. Some were RKO, Pathe, Desilu, Grant Tinker/Gannett and Selznick International Pictures, which used the building as a background during the opening credits of their motion pictures, making the building recognizable to millions of motion picture fans worldwide.

This complex became etched in motion picture history on December 10, 1938, when its entire back lot was turned into Civil War Atlanta, Georgia, and burned to the ground in a lengthy scene for the 1939 motion picture *Gone with the Wind*. In the scene, Rhett Butler (Clark Gable) saves Scarlett O'Hara (Vivien Leigh) by leading her horse-drawn buggy through flames to safety.

The following motion pictures were filmed, in part, at this 17-acre, 14-soundstage production facility.

Opposite: **The Columbia Pictures Entertainment Studios (Culver Studios), 9336 W. Washington Boulevard, California. (Photograph taken in 1986.)**

« King Kong »

This 1933 motion picture was previously addressed in the Auditoriums chapter.
The studio and the back lot were used for several scenes in this film.

« Citizen Kane »

Internationally recognized as one of the ten best motion pictures ever made, this 1941 film relates the rise of a millionaire publisher from humble beginnings to astronomical heights, not only in publishing but politics as well.
Millionaire publisher William Randolph Hearst did his best to keep this motion picture from being made because it closely resembled his life.
Orson Welles starred in and directs the film, quite an accomplishment for the 25-year-old radio performer.
Many interior scenes were filmed at this studio.

« Bugsy »

This 1991 motion picture was previously addressed in the City Halls chapter of this book.
Several scenes were shot at this studio.

« Hook »

The studio complex is a location for many interior scenes in this 1991 movie based on the James Barrie story of the fictional Peter Pan.
Robin Williams stars as a present-day businessman who takes the role of Peter Pan to save his children, who were kidnapped by the evil Capt. Hook (Dustin Hoffman).
The Columbia Pictures Entertainment Studios complex is located at 9336 W. Washington Boulevard, at the intersection of Ince Boulevard in Culver City, south of the Santa Monica Freeway (10). Map Code: 672 H1.

METRO-GOLDWYN-MAYER STUDIOS (CULVER CITY)

The Metro-Goldwyn-Mayer Studios (Sony Corporation/Columbia Studios) began producing features in 1924 and continued at an increasing rate well into the 1930s, when it was considered the premier motion picture studio in the industry.

The 117-acre complex churned out hundreds of motion pictures, many of which are considered classics today and are far too many to mention.

There are several entrances to the studio, two of which are familiar to moviegoers around the world. They are the "classic" entrance and the "art deco" entrance.

The studio complex is much smaller today than during its heyday and has changed owners many times. To those with a love for the Golden Days of Hollywood and for motion picture history, however, the studio will always be known simply as M-G-M.

A few of the motion pictures and television series filmed, in part, at this studio are listed below.

« Anchors Aweigh »

The plot of this 1945 motion picture was previously addressed in the Amphitheater chapter.

The art deco entrance (The Irving Thalberg Building) is a location twice during this film. In one scene Frank Sinatra attempts to enter the studio to talk to Jose Iturbi but is rejected; later in the film, Gene Kelly joins Sinatra in front of the building and the two finally gain entry into the studio.

« Till the Clouds Roll By »

A stirring tribute to songwriter Jerome Kern, the score of this 1946 biography is filled with Kern's songs, all performed by a host of stars, including Judy Garland and Kathryn Grayson. Robert Walker stars as Kern.

MOVIE STUDIOS

The classic entrance to the old M-G-M Studios, 10202 W. Washington Boulevard, Culver City, California. (Photograph taken in 1986.)

The classic entrance on Washington Boulevard is a primary location in the film.

« That's Entertainment »

The first entry in a trilogy of motion pictures saluting musicals produced at this studio, this 1947 film has former stars Fred Astaire, Mickey Rooney and many others as hosts, taking the viewer on a nostalgic trip through studio history.

Scenes from nearly 100 musicals are shown, featuring some of the brightest stars in the motion picture industry.

The classic entrance to the studio is in the opening segment of this film.

The art deco entrance to the Irving Thalberg Building at M-G-M Studios, on Grant Avenue, west of Madison Avenue in Culver City, California. (Photograph taken in 1989.)

« *The Elizabeth Taylor Story* »

This 1995 motion picture was previously addressed in the Hotels chapter.

The classic entrance is in one lengthy scene.

« *I Love Lucy* » *(1951–1957)*

This famous television series was previously addressed in the Houses chapter.

In episode #126, "Ricky Needs an Agent," which was filmed on April 7, 1955, and shown nationally on May 16, 1955, Lucy (Lucille Ball) decides

132　*Movie Studios*

that Ricky (Desi Arnaz) needs an agent to boost his film career at M-G-M. After deciding to represent her husband (Ricky is unaware of this), Lucy goes to the studio to discuss the matter with a studio executive (Parley Baer), which leads to Ricky being released from his contract with the studio.

The art deco entrance of the studio is where Lucy enters to meet with the executive.

This studio is also the location for interior scenes of the *Dallas* television series.

One extremely large building (studio) on the back lot contained an exact replica (full-size) of the South Fork residence of the Ewing family, complete with a garage area and a swimming pool.

All exterior shots of South Fork, a sprawling ranch in Braddock County outside of Dallas, Texas, is an actual ranch home in the Dallas area and is used with the permission of the owners of the property.

The studio complex is bordered by Washington Boulevard, Culver Boulevard, Overland Avenue and Madison Avenue.

The classic entrance to the studio is located at 10202 W. Washington Boulevard.

The art deco entrance is the main entrance of the Irving Thalberg Building, located on the south side of Grant Avenue, west of Madison Avenue.

All locations are in Culver City, California, and are south of the Santa Monica Freeway (10). Map Code: 672 G1.

Paramount Studios (Hollywood)

The only major studio remaining in Hollywood and still producing and releasing motion pictures and television series, Paramount Studios, today has two primary entrances: the "new" entrance, located at 5555 Melrose Avenue, and the "classic" entrance, located a short distance east at the end of Bronson Avenue, north of Melrose. Map Code: 593 G6.

For decades the classic entrance was used by the studio as a location for many of their motion picture productions, making the entrance recognizable to millions of moviegoers worldwide.

When the studio expanded over a decade ago, it engulfed the majority of the acreage of its next door neighbor, R-K-O Radio Pictures Studios, and constructed the new entrance to the complex, retaining the same arched look. However, the original entrance remains a favorite of the thousands of tourists who visit Hollywood movie studios annually.

The vast majority of motion pictures that featured the classic studio entrance were produced by Paramount Studios for the simple reason that such exposure was a great advertising ploy. Other studios using this location, however, placed another name over the entrance.

Segments of the following motion pictures and television series were filmed at this location, using the classic studio entrance as a background.

« *Star Spangled Rhythm* »

This World War II motion picture, released in 1942, has virtually every star at Paramount Studios appearing in a cameo role. The slim plot revolves around a switchboard operator (Betty Hutton), a security guard (Victor Moore) and a sailor (Eddie Bracken) who believes his father (Moore) is the boss of the studio and plans a visit during shore leave.

Moore's guard office is at the entrance, and the entrance is a regular location throughout the film.

« *Variety Girl* »

In another thin plot with appearances by a host of Paramount Studios stars, this 1947 motion picture centers on two girls (Mary Hatcher and Olga San Juan) who come to Hollywood and attempt to get in the movies. This film, a black-and-white release, includes a Puppetoon animated segment in color.

The two girls go in and out of the entrance many times throughout the film.

« *Career* »

This 1959 drama stars Dean Martin and Anthony Franciosa in the story of an actor (Franciosa) whose driving determination gains him fame on the Broadway stage. Carolyn Jones costars as a talent agent.

134 MOVIE STUDIOS

The classic entrance to Paramount Studios, 5555 Melrose Avenue, Hollywood, California. (Photograph taken in 1988.)

« *The Day of the Locust* »

Nathanael West's powerful novel about 1930s Hollywood virtually comes to life in this 1975 motion picture. The revealing plot centers on an artist (William Atherton) who somehow finds the glamour of Hollywood in the variety of unusual characters he encounters. Donald Sutherland and Karen Black are outstanding costars in this film.

The studio entrance is a location in several scenes.

« *Won Ton Ton, the Dog Who Saved Hollywood* »

The studio was transformed into the "Mack Sennett Studios" in this 1976 motion picture that spoofs 1920s Hollywood. The plot centers on the rise, fall and rise of a dog who became a superstar in the silent film era. Bruce Dern and a host of Hollywood stars are featured.

The studio entrance is in several scenes.

« *There Must Be a Pony* »

Elizabeth Taylor portrays a movie star attempting a comeback after her release from a mental hospital. Robert Wagner co-stars in this 1986 film. The studio entrance is a location in several scenes.

« *The Elizabeth Taylor Story* »

This 1995 motion picture was previously addressed in the Hotels chapter and in this chapter.

As with the films previously listed, the studio entrance is prominent in several scenes.

« *The Phil Silvers Show* »
(1955–1959)

A top sitcom in the 1950s, this television series was originally titled "You'll Never Get Rich" but switched titles shortly after it first aired on September 20, 1955.

Comedian Phil Silvers stars as Master Sergeant Ernie Bilko, a military con artist who has a heart of gold.

In a first season episode, Bilko (Silvers) is sent to a Hollywood movie studio by Army brass to serve as a technical advisor for a single battle scene that recreated a battle fought on a Pacific island during World War II that Bilko's unit was engaged in.

This studio is the "C.D. Chadwick Production" studio, and its owner, Mr. Chadwick (Howard Smith), is nearly pushed to insanity as Bilko continually disrupts production, finally causing the film to be cancelled.

HAL ROACH STUDIOS (CULVER CITY)

The Hal Roach Studios were previously addressed in the Car Lots chapter of this book.

Major motion pictures and television series produced at this location but not previously addressed are discussed below.

136   Movie Studios

Hal Roach Studios site, 8822 W. Washington Boulevard, Culver City, California. (Photograph taken in 1995.)

« Sons of the Desert »

    Considered by the majority of Laurel and Hardy fans worldwide as the comedy team's finest effort, this 1933 motion picture, their 75th film together and their 42nd "talkie," has Laurel and Hardy planning to go to Chicago, Illinois, to attend a convention held by their lodge, the Los Angeles Oasis 13 of the Sons of the Desert. To do this, the two must get permission from their wives (Mae Busch and Dorothy Christy). Stan does and Ollie doesn't, and the two spin a web of lies to go on the trip.
    The majority of the film was shot at this studio, with the only stock footage used being a newsreel clip showing the Santa Monica Lodge of Elks marching in sharp cadence, participating in a parade.

« Of Mice and Men »

Author John Steinbeck's powerful novel is brought to the screen in this 1939 film starring Burgess Meredith as a migrant worker who floats from job to job in Central California with his friend, Lennie (Lon Chaney, Jr.), a feeble-minded hulk with the strength of ten men. Meredith is not only Chaney's pal but his caretaker as he continually protects him throughout a myriad of trying situations during the film.

Location shooting was done in Central California in and near the town of Weed, and interior scenes were filmed at this studio.

« The Abbott and Costello Show » (1952)

Comedians Bud Abbott and Lou Costello brought many of their burlesque routines to television in this series that lasted for only 52 episodes, all of which were filmed at this studio.

« Blondie » (1957)

This television adaptation of the long-running motion picture series (1938–1950) and Chic Young's comic strip stars Pamela Britton as Blondie and Arthur Lake (who played Dagwood in the motion picture series) as Dagwood.

All episodes were filmed at this studio.

« Racket Squad » (1950–1953)

One of the first crime series to appear on television, Reed Hadley stars as Captain John Braddock of San Francisco's elite "Racket Squad," a group of cops who single out and eventually track down con artists.

This series was filmed, in part, at this studio.

The site of the Hal Roach Studios (now the location of a car dealership) is 8822 W. Washington Boulevard in Culver City, California, south of the Santa Monica Freeway (10). Map Code: 632 H7.

SENNETT STUDIOS (LOS ANGELES)

The Sennett Studios, affectionately known in the motion picture industry as the "Fun Factory," opened in 1912 and were managed by motion picture pioneer Mack Sennett. One of the first motion picture studios in Los Angeles, Sennett produced hundreds of silent comedies starring a host of actors.

The size of studio property has been greatly reduced over the decades, and today only one building remains. In the past it served as a roller rink, a Western dance hall and as a storage facility for the scenery and wardrobe for a local theater group.

The studio building is #256 in the city's Historic-Cultural Monuments listing and is located at 1712 Glendale Boulevard, north of the Hollywood Freeway (101). Map Code: 594 E6.

The only remaining building of the Mack Sennett Studios, located at 1712 Glendale Boulevard, Los Angeles. (Photograph taken in 1986.)

20TH CENTURY–FOX STUDIOS (LOS ANGELES)

The origin of the 20th Century–Fox Studios began when Darryl F. Zanuck left Warner Brothers in 1933, met with independent film producer Joseph Schenck and proposed to form a film company. The rather unusual name of the new studio came during a conversation between Samuel G. Engle, Zanuck's assistant, and Zanuck when Zanuck told Engle he wanted a name for the new company and Engel replied that any name would have to be good for 67 years. Zanuck asked what the name would be and Engle replied, "Twentieth Century Pictures."

The original gated entrance to the 20th Century–Fox Studios, Tennessee Street and Fox Hills Drive, Los Angeles, California. (Photograph taken in 1989.)

A later merger with William Fox, head of the Fox Film Corporation, in 1935 added the "Fox" name to this now famous title.

Two popular stars, Will Rogers and 7-year-old Shirley Temple, carried the studio through the first year. Rogers died in an airplane crash in 1935 outside Barrow, Alaska, but Temple continued under contract to the studio, starring in hit after hit.

The original "old" gated entrance to the studio complex was, of course, used by scores of major stars over several decades. When the entrance was moved to 10201 W. Pico Boulevard, on the opposite side of the complex, the original entrance was closed, but it was used as a location in later motion picture and television series productions.

« L.A. Law »
(1986–1994)

This television series was previously addressed in the Buildings chapter of this book.

The original gated entrance to the studio is a location in a 1992 episode.

The original ("old") gated entrance to the studio is located at the terminus of Tennessee Street, east of Fox Hills Drive and north of the Santa Monica Freeway (10) in Los Angeles. Map Code: 632 E4.

UNIVERSAL PICTURES STUDIOS
(UNIVERSAL CITY)

When Universal City opened on March 15, 1915, it became the only city in the world built exclusively to house facilities for motion picture production. This city became the home of the Universal Film Manufacturing Company, now known as Universal Pictures Studios.

The president of the studio, Carl Laemmle, selected the name when he saw a wagon on the street in front of his New York City office with the words "Universal Pipe Fittings" painted on its side. To date, well over 3,000 motion pictures and scores of television series productions have been made and released by this studio, but it has become more famous as a major tourist attraction.

MOVIE STUDIOS 141

The railroad station at Universal Studios, a film location for over 70 years. The station serves as the background for the closing scenes in Abbott and Costello's 1943 film, *Hit the Ice*. (Photograph taken in 1986.)

A producer of major motion pictures for well over a decade, Universal Studios became world famous in the early 1930s with the release of *Dracula* and *Frankenstein*, both in 1931, and *The Mummy* in 1932. Sequels followed well past the end of World War II in 1945.

Many of the films were shot, in part, in the "European Streets" set, which was constructed in 1931 specifically for the *Frankenstein* motion picture. Within this area is a town square, complete with a fountain.

A bit farther away is the house (often referred to as a mansion) seen in the *Psycho* motion picture series. Close to this house is the infamous "Bates Motel," the location where Anthony Perkins (portraying Norman Bates) slashed Janet Leigh to death in the now classic shower scene in the 1960 motion picture *Psycho*.

142 MOVIE STUDIOS

Universal's "Bates Mansion," a location in the first three *Psycho* motion pictures and in a 1994 episode of television's *The Adventures of Brisco County, Jr.* (Photograph taken in 1986.)

« *The Adventures of Brisco County, Jr.* » *(1993–1994)*

This television series was previously addressed in the Caves chapter of this book.

In an episode that aired nationally on April 29, 1994, the mansion is a boarding house/funeral parlor in a comedic re-creation of the *Psycho* shower scene.

Universal Studio's railroad station is located near the European Streets area. A rail line runs in front of it for a short distance as a track for a variety of railroad vehicles necessary for scenes of motion picture or television series production.

« *Hit the Ice* »

A skating rink in Sun Valley, Idaho, is the centerpiece in this 1943 motion picture starring Bud Abbott and Lou Costello as newspaper photographers involved with a gang of crooks while attempting to recover money taken in a bank robbery.

The railroad station is prominent in a closing scene of the film where Lou Costello is hooked to the rear car of a train by a station mail bag device.

Universal Studios is located at 100 Universal City Plaza, north of the Hollywood Freeway (101) in Universal City, California. Map Code: 563 B6.

Observatories

Griffith Observatory (Los Angeles)

GRIFFITH OBSERVATORY (LOS ANGELES)

The Griffith Observatory, located in the vastness of Griffith Park in Los Angeles, was a gift to the city of Colonel Griffith J. Griffith to allow the public access to the wonders of astronomy and modern science.

The complex, an outstanding example of the art deco design style popular in the 1930s, opened on May 14, 1935, and is #168 in the city's Historic-Cultural Monuments listing.

Segments of the following motion pictures, serials and television series productions were filmed at this location.

« *The Amazing Colossal Man* »

Glenn Langan stars as a U.S. Army officer who survives an atomic explosion and begins to grow, reaching the "amazing" height of 60 feet. Langan then attacks Las Vegas, Nevada, and also the Griffith Observatory, where he encounters the wrath of the military in this 1957 sci-fi classic.

« Criminal Behavior »

Based on author Ross MacDonald's *The Ferguson Affair*, this 1992 movie features Farrah Fawcett as a defense lawyer dodging a killer while trying to find evidence in a complex murder case in Los Angeles.

« Love Can Be Murder »

Jaclyn Smith plays a present-day private investigator who enters a dream sequence and travels back to 1940s Los Angeles in this 1992 motion picture. There she meets the ghost (Corbin Bernsen) of a murdered private investigator who won't let her alone until she helps him solve his murder.

« Devil in a Blue Dress »

This 1992 film takes place in 1948 Los Angeles and stars Denzel Washington as Easy Rawlings, an out-of-work man who helps a criminal find the former fiancée of a man running for the office of mayor.

« Her Last Chance »

Kellie Martin stars as a teenager charged and indicted for a murder in this 1996 motion picture. Patti LuPone portrays Martin's mother, who tries desperately to get her daughter off alcohol and drugs, and free of the murder charge.

The observatory is in one lengthy scene in this film.

« House of Frankenstein 1997 »

Dr. Frankenstein's monster (Peter Crombie) is located in the Arctic ice and brought to Los Angeles, where he is joined by a vampire and a werewolf and terrorizes the city.

The observatory is the location of a party near the opening of the film where a werewolf attacks a couple walking from the building toward

The Griffith Observatory, located at 2800 E. Observatory Road, Los Angeles, California, is frequently seen in film segments. (Photograph taken in 1986.)

a parking lot. The observatory is also the location of the police investigation relating to the attack.

The House of Frankenstein? It is a nightclub that is burned to the ground in the closing scenes of this 1997 film.

« *Flash Gordon* »

The observatory is in several of the 13 chapters of this 1936 serial starring Larry "Buster" Crabbe as Flash Gordon and Jean Rogers as Dale Arden.

In this first Flash Gordon serial (*Flash Gordon's Trip to Mars* [1938] and *Flash Gordon Conquers the Universe* [1940] complete the trio of serials), the Planet Mongo is hurling through outer space to collide with earth. Flash, Dale and Dr. Zarkov (Frank Shannon) jump in a rocket ship and head toward Mongo to prevent disaster.

After 12 harrowing escapes from the evil Emperor Ming (Charles Middleton), Flash, Dale and Dr. Zarkov save Mongo and head back to Earth.

« *Flash Gordon Conquers the Universe* »

The final Flash Gordon serial, this 1940 entry has Flash (Larry "Buster" Crabbe) heading back to the planet Mongo with Dale (Carol Hughes) and Dr. Zarkov (Frank Shannon) to again confront Emperor Ming (Charles Middleton) to stop the spread of the Plague of the Purple Death, a death dust Ming has spread in the Earth's atmosphere.

The observatory is once again in several chapters.

« *The Purple Monster Strikes* »

The observatory appears throughout this 15-chapter serial released in 1945.

In the plot, a meteor lands near the observatory. Seeing this, Dr. Layton (James Craven) investigates and is met by a Martian (Roy Barcroft) sent to Earth in the meteor to meet Dr. Layton and get his plans for a spacecraft that will travel to Mars and bring Martians back to Earth to conquer it. Barcroft eventually takes off in the spaceship toward Mars and is destroyed by a ray gun fired by the hero, Craig Foster (Dennis Moore).

« *Cannon* » *(1971–1976)*

Frank Cannon (William Conrad), a former cop turned private eye, was the only star in the series' 124 episodes.

In one episode, he investigates a murder at this observatory.

« *Players* »
(1997–1998)

The plot of this television series was previously addressed in the City Halls chapter.

The observatory is a location in the October 24, 1997, episode, "Con Law," where Frank John Hughes met with a crooked attorney in an F.B.I. sting that didn't work.

The Griffith Observatory is located in Griffith Park at 2800 E. Observatory Road, north of Los Feliz Boulevard and west of the Golden State Freeway (5) in Los Angeles, California. Map Code: 593 J2.

Parks

Arboretum of Los Angeles County (Arcadia)
Griffith Park (Los Angeles)
Pershing Square (Los Angeles)
Placerita Canyon State Park (Newhall)
Plaza Park (Los Angeles)
Vasquez Rocks County Park (Agua Dulce)

Parks of all sizes, from one of the smallest, Media Park, to one of the largest, Placerita Canyon State Park, have been used as locations for motion pictures and television series dating back to the 1920s.

ARBORETUM OF LOS ANGELES COUNTY (ARCADIA)

Although not technically a park, the Arboretum of Los Angeles County, a 127-acre complex, boasts many parklike attractions, such as the Australian, Mediterranean, and South American sections. It has lagoons and jungle areas that have proved to be favorite locations for scores of motion pictures and television series productions since 1937.

Before the property was acquired by the State of California and County of Los Angeles in 1947, the arboretum was owned by a real estate syndicate, the Harry Chandler Rancho Santa Anita, Inc.

Many of the major motion pictures and television series filmed at this location are listed in the Lakes chapter of this book.

The Arboretum of Los Angeles County is located at 301 N. Baldwin Avenue, south of the Foothill Freeway (210) in Arcadia, California. Map Code: 567 A5.

GRIFFITH PARK (LOS ANGELES)

Griffith Park, northwest of the downtown area of the city of Los Angeles, is one of the largest parks located within the city limits of a metropolitan area, comparable to Central Park in New York City and Swope Park in Kansas City, Missouri.

The north border of the park is roughly Riverside Drive and the Ventura Freeway (134); the east border, the Los Angeles River and the Golden State Freeway (5); the west border, Beachwood Drive and Forest Lawn Drive; and the southern border, a large residential area located north of Los Feliz Boulevard.

Within this park are the Griffith Observatory and Bronson Canyon (and the caves of the canyon). Many motion pictures and television series filmed at these locations are addressed in the Caves and the Observatory chapters of this book. Map Code: 593 J2.

PERSHING SQUARE (LOS ANGELES)

Pershing Square, dense with trees, plants and grass, is a green jewel situated in the cement canyons of the downtown Los Angeles area, and it provides a friendly bit of nature for thousands of workers from nearby buildings as well as the many tourists who visit this small park daily.

Several scenes from the following motion picture were filmed in and near this park.

The 5th Street and Hill Street entrance to Pershing Square in downtown Los Angeles, the location of a kidnapping scene in the 1994 motion picture *Speed*. (Photograph taken in 1998.)

« *Speed* »

The plot of this 1994 motion picture was previously addressed in the City Halls chapter.

This park is the location where Keanu Reeves' costar, Sandra Bullock, is kidnapped by Dennis Hopper and where Reeves discovers Hopper's secret entrance to the Pershing Square Subway Station where Bullock is being held captive with sticks of dynamite strapped to her body.

Pershing Square is bounded by 5th Street, 6th Street, Hill Street and Olive Street in downtown Los Angeles. Map Code: 634 E4 & F4.

Placerita Canyon State Park (Newhall)

The Placerita Canyon State Park will be addressed in the Ranches chapter of this book.

The park is located on Placerita Canyon Road, 1¼ miles east of the Antelope Valley Freeway (14) and north of the Golden State Freeway (5), near the city of Newhall, California. Map Code: 4641 G1.

Plaza Park (Los Angeles)

The Plaza Park in downtown Los Angeles is a small part of the original Pueblo Land Grant. It was near this location on September 4, 1781, that the city of Los Angeles was founded by 11 families on the orders of Governor Felipe de Neve.

The park, the surrounding buildings and the adjoining Olvera Street are major tourist attractions as well as a favorite location for production companies.

The following motion picture and television series segments were filmed at this location.

« Lethal Weapon 3 »

Danny Glover, a cop ready to retire, is once again teamed with his out-of-control partner (Mel Gibson) to investigate a series of crimes by an ex-cop in this 1992 motion picture.

This park is the scene of an armored car robbery.

Opposite: Plaza Park in downtown Los Angeles, looking north toward historic Olvera Street. (Photograph taken in 1998.)

« Amazing Stories » (1985–1987)

The plot of this television series was previously addressed in the Buildings chapter of this book.

The Plaza Park is a location in the "Alamo Jobe" episode that first aired nationally in 1985. The park is seen as Jobe (Kelly Reno) steps from the Alamo structure in 1836 and into the park in 1985 San Antonio, Texas.

Plaza Park, Historic-Cultural Monument #64, is located in downtown Los Angeles, north of the Hollywood Freeway (101), between Main Street and Alameda Street. Map Code: 634 G3.

VASQUEZ ROCKS COUNTY PARK (AGUA DULCE)

The Vasquez Rocks County Park in the Santa Clarita Valley area of Los Angeles County has an enormous 20-million-year-old rock formation that has served as a hideout for outlaws in the late 1800s and as a location for motion picture and television series productions for the past six decades.

A clever camera angle transforms the rock formation and the adjacent desert area into an alien planet, a desolate area in a foreign country or a part of the American West.

The following motion pictures and television series were filmed, in part, at or near this rock formation.

« Werewolf of London »

The first film addressing werewolves, this 1935 motion picture stars Henry Hull as a scientist who is bitten by a werewolf, becomes one himself, and goes on a killing spree in London, England.

The rock formation is a section of Tibet where Hull, in search of an exotic flower, is attacked and bitten by a werewolf.

« Colorado »

Roy Rogers and George "Gabby" Hayes star as a Union Army lieutenant and his sidekick who ride past the rock formation en route to Denver, Colorado, to investigate a problem with the Indians in this 1940 motion picture.

« The Man from Oklahoma »

Roy Rogers and George "Gabby" Hayes are a team again in this 1945 motion picture and again at the rock formation in this Western adventure wherein the two investigate a feud between rival ranchers.

« Fury of the Congo »

Johnny Weissmuller stars as Jungle Jim, a hero based on the comic book and radio show character in this 1951 motion picture, the 6th entry in the 16 film series.

As the film opens, Jim encounters smugglers who are in Africa searching for the wild Okongo, an animal whose secretions form a potent narcotic.

The rocks are the site of a desperate fight near the conclusion of the film as Jim and friendly natives defeat the smugglers as a sandstorm rages.

« Kung Fu »

This 1972 movie was the pilot film for the 1972–1975 television series of the same title starring David Carradine as a martial-arts expert who comes to the Old West in the 1800s to champion the rights of Chinese coolies who are continually exploited by many businessmen.

« Blazing Saddles »

The rock formation and the nearby area are locations in this 1974 spoof of Western films. Clevon Little stars as the new black sheriff of a

The rock formation at Vasquez Rocks County Park, a location in scores of films. (Photograph taken in 1986.)

town who hired him sight unseen and expected a white sheriff to fill the vacancy.

« *The Flintstones* »

Based on William Hanna and Joseph Barbera's television cartoon series of the same title (1960–1966/1981), which was the first prime-time cartoon series made especially for television, this 1994 live-action motion picture stars John Goodman as Fred Flintstone and Elizabeth Perkins as his wife, Wilma, with motion picture legend Elizabeth Taylor as Fred's mother-in-law.

The plot centers on Fred's promotion at his firm, Slate and Company, and his wrenching decision to fire his buddy, Barney (Rick Moranis), who is accused of theft.

The town of Bedrock, the home of the Flintstones, was constructed in front of the rock formation.

« *The Invaders* »

The plot of this 1995 motion picture was previously addressed in the Bridges chapter.
The rock formation is one of many Los Angeles area locations seen throughout this film.

« *Friends Till the End* »

A delusional college girl slowly becomes totally obsessed with assuming the life of her classmate (Shannen Doherty).
The rock formation is a location in two scenes in this 1997 motion picture.

« *Lassie* »
(1954–1974)

The resourceful collie, Lassie, survived for two decades in this television series. Six dogs played the lead role and a host of actors portrayed the dog's owners, neighbors, bad guys and good guys in regular and occasional roles.
The rock formation is a location in a 1960s episode wherein Lassie meets a wallaby.

« *77th Bengal Lancers* »
(1956–1957)

This television adventure series is set in India. Warren Stevens stars as Lt. Rhodes, who is stationed at Fort Oghora, the principal location in this series.
The television production company constructed the fort in front of the rock formation.

« Sliders »
(1995–)

This sci-fi television series, set in San Francisco, sends principal characters, led by Quinn Mallory (Jerry O'Connell), into a "wormhole" and to adventures in different worlds, all in the same geographic location—San Francisco.

In an October 1996 episode, the area in front of the rock formation is the setting of a desert village that was plagued by tornadoes and ruled by a dictator.

The Vasquez Rocks County Park is located north of the Antelope Valley Freeway (14), at the intersection of Schafer Road and Agua Dulce Canyon Road in Agua Dulce, California. Map Code: 4463 E2.

Piers

Marina Del Rey (Los Angeles)
Santa Monica Pier (Santa Monica)

A pier, dock or a marina, in essence, is a location where boats and ships of varying sizes arrive or depart, carrying an assortment of merchandise or passengers.

As the western boundaries of many of the communities that make up greater Los Angeles, including Los Angeles itself, terminate at the Pacific Ocean, a wide variety of piers, docks and marinas are present. Many are regularly used as locations for production companies.

Segments of the following motion pictures and television series were filmed at the below listed locations.

MARINA DEL REY (LOS ANGELES)

The Marina Del Rey section of Los Angeles with its many docking basins and Fisherman's Village is a very popular tourist attraction as well as a functional marina for hundreds of boat owners.

The Marina Del Rey pier area and the Marina Del Rey Channel, a frequent film location. (Photograph taken in 1988.)

« *Obsessive Love* »

The docking area and the Mariner's Statue of the marina are locations in this 1984 motion picture featuring Simon MacCorkindale as a television soap-opera star who is the victim of a disturbed fan (Yvette Mimieux) trying to seduce him and ruin his marriage.

« *Kids Don't Tell* »

Michael Ontkean stars as a film producer whose documentary on the crime of the sexual abuse of children begins to destroy his home life in this 1985 film. Ontkean met a friend on a boat that was docked at this marina to discuss the film project.

The Mariner's Statue overlooking the Marina Del Rey pier area, another frequent film location. (Photograph taken in 1986.)

« *Kidnapped* »

The docking area and the Mariner's Statue are the locations of a police chase and shoot-out in this 1987 motion picture that centers on a policeman (David Naughton) who helps a woman (Barbara Crampton) rescue her teenage sister (Kim Evenson) from filmmakers who specialize in pornography.

Marina Del Rey is located north of Culver Boulevard, west of Lincoln Boulevard and west of the San Diego Freeway (405). Map Code: 702 B1.

Santa Monica Pier (Santa Monica)

The Santa Monica Pier is more than a pier; it borders on amusement park status with its electric car ride and merry-go-round. The pier is also the site of the once-magnificent Santa Monica Ballroom.

It is not surprising, then, that this seaside location has been and continues to be a favorite location of production companies.

Segments of the following motion pictures and television series were filmed on or adjacent to this pier.

« *The Glenn Miller Story* »

The plot of this 1954 motion picture was previously addressed in the Alleys chapter.

In a lengthy scene in the film, Miller (James Stewart) is frustrated that his musical talent is not fully appreciated by orchestra leader Ben Pollack (playing himself) and walks from a ballroom (the building will be addressed later in this chapter) and onto the pier. Miller's friend, Chummy (Harry Morgan), runs after him and brings him back to the ballroom when Pollack has a change of mind.

« *Hot Moves* »

The pier is a location in the opening scenes of this 1984 beach movie, featuring Michael Zorek and Adam Silbar as two of four California surfers who go on a crusade to lose their virginity before summer's end.

« *Victim of Love* »

A romantic mystery, this 1991 motion picture stars JoBeth Williams as a psychologist and Virginia Madsen as her patient. The two become deeply involved with the same man (Pierce Brosnan).

The pier is a location in one lengthy scene in this film.

The area of the Santa Monica Pier seen in many motion pictures and television series sequences. (Photograph taken in 1986.)

« The Net »

Complications that could arise from the increasing use of computers are starkly evident in this suspenseful 1995 film wherein Sandra Bullock's identity is stolen and her murder planned after she receives a computer disc.

The pier is the location of one of many attempts on her life.

The Santa Monica Ballroom was located on the south side of the pier, just past the merry-go-round and the electric car ride, and is noted as the location of three scenes in the following motion picture.

« The Glenn Miller Story »

The plot of this 1954 motion picture was previously addressed in the Alleys chapter and a location on this pier was addressed earlier in this chapter.

The Santa Monica Pier's electric car ride, a frequent film location. (Photograph taken in 1986.)

The ballroom serves as the location where Miller (James Stewart) tried out with the Ben Pollack Orchestra; a Boston, Massachusetts, dancehall; and the "Glen Island Casino" in the film.

The ballroom also served as a location where the *Spade Cooley Show* was telecast in the 1950s by a local Los Angeles television station. Cooley was the leader of a Western band.

As a note of interest, this ballroom was converted into a roller hockey rink in 1957 and served as the location for semi-pro roller hockey teams whose games were televised locally. The author played on one of these teams.

The electric car ride on the pier served as a location in segments of the following motion picture.

Goalie (author) Leon Smith on his knees in front of the cage after making a "save" in a roller hockey game during the 1957 season at the Santa Monica Ballroom, the location of several scenes in the motion picture *The Glenn Miller Story*, which was filmed three years earlier. (Photograph taken in 1957, from the author's collection.)

« Casualties of Love: The "Long Island Lolita" Story »

This 1993 television movie delves into the events leading to the attack on Mary Jo Buttafuoco (Phyllis Lyons) by teenager Amy Fisher (Alyssa Milano), who allegedly committed the crime to gain the love of Mary Jo's husband, Joseph (Jack Scalia), and the aftermath involving this unusual trio of New Yorkers.

The car ride is a Long Island, New York, electric ride during a Buttafuoco family outing in the film.

As a note of interest, palm trees (none grow wild in New York) are seen in the distance behind Joseph's (Joey's) Long Island auto repair shop.

The merry-go-round located on the pier served as a location for the following motion pictures.

« *Victim of Love* »

The plot of this 1991 film was addressed earlier in this chapter. The merry-go-round is a location in one lengthy scene.

« *Dead Before Dawn* »

The merry-go-round is a part of a Dallas, Texas, amusement park in this fact-based 1993 motion picture starring Cheryl Ladd as a battered wife who files for divorce from her husband (Jameson Parker), an action that prompts him to arrange her murder.

« *Rescue Me* »

In this 1993 movie, a troubled high-school boy (Stephen Dorff) finds a biker (Michael Dudikoff) and embarks on a personal crusade to rescue a cute cheerleader kidnapped by a gang led by Peter DeLuise.

The merry-go-round on the pier is the location near the end of the film where Dorff finds the cheerleader.

The pier's parking area, located immediately north of the pier, is also a location seen in motion pictures.

« *Beverly Hills Cop III* »

The plot of this 1994 action-comedy was previously addressed in the City Halls chapter.

Eddie Murphy, on the trail of killers, locates their truck parked in this parking area.

« *Species* »

This 1995 sci-fi-horror motion picture exposes a DNA experiment that went wrong, producing a rapidly aging half human, half alien

(Natasha Henstridge) who escapes from a United States government laboratory in Dugway, Utah, and ends up in Los Angeles. Her sole purpose is to mate as rapidly as possible to perpetuate her species.

The parking area of the pier is where Henstridge awakes in a stolen car after killing a man miles away and taking his car.

The Santa Monica Pier is located at the end of Colorado Avenue, west of Ocean Avenue, in Santa Monica, California. Map Code: 671 E3.

Police Stations

Highland Park Police Station (Los Angeles)
Los Angeles Police Academy (Los Angeles)
Parker Center Police Headquarters (Los Angeles)

The Los Angeles Police Department has 18 geographic police divisions, each with its own station. Some of these stations, constructed in the 1920s and 1930s, are gradually being replaced by more modern and functional buildings. Most of the older stations have been demolished, but some have not.

As with other buildings across the greater Los Angeles landscape utilized as locations for segments of motion picture and television series productions, police stations are regularly included.

The following Los Angeles Police Department facilities and sites have been and continue to be locations for varied scenes.

HIGHLAND PARK POLICE STATION (LOS ANGELES)

The Highland Park Police Station, located in the Highland Park District of Los Angeles, was affectionately known as "Old #11" by neighborhood residents and police officers assigned there. Closed decades ago

POLICE STATIONS

The old Highland Park Police Station, located at 6045 York Boulevard, Los Angeles, is frequently seen in motion picture and television series segments. (Photograph taken in 1986.)

and replaced by a modern facility nearby, this station was retained in its original condition as an historical monument (#274 in the city's Historic-Cultural Monuments listing). Since its closing, the building is regularly used as a location (primarily interior) for motion picture and television series production segments.

The building is currently being renovated and will soon become the home of the Los Angeles Police Historical Society Museum.

« Police Academy 6: City Under Siege »

The plot of this 1989 motion picture was previously addressed in the Bridges chapter of this book.

The building is a police station in the film.

« *The Invaders* »

The plot of this 1995 motion picture was also previously addressed in the Bridges chapter. The building served as a police station.

« *Once You Meet a Stranger* »

The building is the Santa Mira Police Station in this 1996 motion picture, which is strikingly similar to Alfred Hitchcock's 1951 thriller *Strangers on a Train*. In this film, however, the gender roles are reversed, as the chance meeting of two women (Jacqueline Bisset and Theresa Russell) results in murder and the expectation of murder.

« *Major Dad* » *(1989–1993)*

Gerald McRaney stars as Marine Corps Major J.D. "Mac" MacGillis, and Shanna Reed stars as his wife, Polly, in this television series revolving around life on a variety of military bases.

This building is a police station in several episodes of the series.

The old Highland Park Police Station is located at 6045 York Boulevard, near Figueroa Street, west of the Pasadena Freeway (110). Map Code: 595 D1.

LOS ANGELES POLICE ACADEMY (LOS ANGELES)

The Los Angeles Police Academy, a police facility that does not provide services to a particular community of the city, does, however, train police officers prior to their taking the field in fleets of black-and-white police vehicles.

This massive facility is a popular location for motion picture and television series production companies.

The main entrance to the Los Angeles Police Academy, 1880 N. Academy Drive, near downtown Los Angeles. (Photograph taken in 1987.)

« *The Rockford Files: Friends and Foul Play* »

The plot of this 1996 television movie was previously addressed in the Hospitals chapter of this book.
This facility is the location of one lengthy segment in the film.

« *On the Line* »

The plot of this 1998 motion picture was previously addressed in the Buildings chapter.
This facility is the location where, in two scenes, Linda Hamilton jogged to keep in shape. The entrance and the athletic field are prominent in these scenes.

The Los Angeles Police Academy is located at 1880 N. Academy Drive in Elysian Park, across the street from Dodger Stadium. There is an Academy Drive exit on both the northbound and southbound lanes of the nearby Pasadena Freeway (110). Academy Road leads to Academy Drive. Map Code: 594 G6.

Parker Center Police Headquarters (Los Angeles)

A tourist attraction, a primary location for motion picture and television series production companies, and the target of vandals during the infamous Los Angeles riots of 1992, Parker Center Police Headquarters is the police department's administration building, made famous by actor Jack Webb's television series, *Dragnet*, soon after the building was dedicated on September 12, 1955. Originally the Police Administration Building, it was renamed in memory of the last chief of police, William H. Parker.

Segments of the following productions were filmed at this facility.

« Dead Ringer »

Bette Davis has a dual role as identical twin sisters (Edith and Margaret) in this 1964 motion picture. Jealous over Margaret's wealth and success in life, Edith murders her and takes her identity and lifestyle. Karl Malden is the police detective who investigates the crime. As the film ends, Edith receives the death penalty.

This building is the police headquarters where Malden is assigned.

« The Case of the Hillside Stranglers »

The plot of this 1989 motion picture was previously addressed in the Courts chapter.

This police facility is the location of the "Hillside Strangler Task Force" where Grogan's (Richard Crenna) office is located.

The main (Los Angeles Street) entrance to Parker Center Police Headquarters. (Photograph taken in 1998.)

« *Columbo: Caution, Murder Can Be Hazardous to Your Health* »

Los Angeles Police Department Detective Lieutenant Columbo (Peter Falk) matches wits with the host of a television crime show (George Hamilton) who murders his rival and attempts to fool Columbo.

The building is the location of Columbo's office.

174 POLICE STATIONS

Parker Center Police Headquarters, located at 150 N. Los Angeles Street in downtown Los Angeles. (Photograph taken in 1998.)

« Land's End »
(1995-   )

The plot of this television series was previously addressed in the City Halls chapter of this book.

The building is the location where Officer Mike Land (Fred Dryer) was assigned when he quit the force and headed for Mexico to hunt for his wife's killer.

« Murder One »
(1995-   )

The plot of this television series was previously addressed in the Courts chapter.

POLICE STATIONS   175

The San Pedro Street entrance to Parker Center Police Headquarters' Jail Division, where Orenthal James Simpson was taken and booked for murder in 1994. (Photograph taken in 1998.)

The building is the location of a police facility during the first episode of the series.

« *Murder, She Wrote* » *(1984–1996)*

This television series was previously addressed in the Caves chapter.

The building serves frequently as a police station throughout this series.

As a note of interest, this building was the focus of worldwide attention when Orenthal James Simpson was brought here, interrogated and later briefly imprisoned when charged for the June 12, 1994, murders of

Nicole Brown and Ron Goldman. He was eventually transferred to the nearby Central Jail, where he remained throughout the subsequent trial.

Parker Center Police Headquarters is located at 150 North Los Angeles Street in downtown Los Angeles, south of the Hollywood Freeway (101) and east of the Harbor Freeway (110). Map Code: 634 G4.

Railroad Stations

Angel's Flight (Los Angeles)
Santa Anita Depot (Arcadia)
Pasadena Train Station (Pasadena)
Santa Fe Railroad Station (Los Angeles)
Union Station (Los Angeles)

Railroad stations, large and small, still exist in the greater Los Angeles area, serving hundreds of thousands of passengers arriving and departing each year and providing a location for thousands of motion picture and television series fans who frequent them to absorb the atmosphere of past and present productions filmed there.

Some railroad stations have been demolished or relocated. One, however, remains fully functional. All will be addressed and many motion picture and television series segments filmed at various locations will be listed.

ANGEL'S FLIGHT (LOS ANGELES)

Angel's Flight (also Angels Flight) in downtown Los Angeles is known worldwide as the "world's shortest railway." This landmark, #4 in the city's Historic-Cultural Monuments listing, is included in this chapter

Railroad Stations

Looking west on 3rd Street toward Hill Street and the 3rd Street Tunnel. The site of the old Angel's Flight is just to the left of the entrance to the tunnel. (Photograph taken in 1998.)

because it has a railroad station, a small structure operated by one person, located at the top of Bunker Hill, where the tracks terminate after the short climb from Hill Street.

Built in 1901, the railway served the public steadily until it closed in 1969 because of extensive construction on Bunker Hill. Originally located on the south side of the 3rd Street Tunnel, at the intersection of 3rd and Hill Streets, the railway was moved to its present location, a short distance south, near 4th and Hill Streets, where it now operates on a daily basis.

The past and present locations of Angel's Flight are regularly seen in travelogs of the Los Angeles area, as well as in vintage newsreels of that area of the city.

Segments of the following motion pictures were filmed on or near Angel's Flight.

Angel's Flight today, looking west from Hill Street toward the top of Bunker Hill and Angel's Flight Station. (Photograph taken in 1998.)

« Night Has a Thousand Eyes »

Edward G. Robinson stars in this 1948 film about a man who can foresee the future and makes a determined effort to save Gail Russell from the hands of a murderer, an effort that costs him his life.

In this film, Robinson lives in a shabby rooming house located on the north side of the 3rd Street Tunnel, just west of the intersection of 3rd and Hill Streets. The old location of Angel's Flight was directly across the entrance to the tunnel from the rooming house, and the railroad's two cars, "Olivet" and "Sinai," are seen several times.

« The Glenn Miller Story »

The plot of this 1954 motion picture was previously addressed in the Alleys chapter.

RAILROAD STATIONS

Angel's Flight Station, a location used in a segment of the 1997 motion picture *Tell Me No Secrets*. (Photograph taken in 1998.)

The old Angel's Flight is a primary location as the film opens. It is across the alley from a pawn shop, the East Los Angeles Loan Company, owned by W. Kranz (Sig Ruman), where Glenn Miller (James Stewart) regularly hocked his trombone to get money for a room and some food.

Angel's Flight is seen several more times in the early part of this motion picture when Miller's friend, "Chummy" (Harry Morgan), meets him to go to a variety of musical engagements.

« *The Indestructible Man* »

The plot of this 1956 thriller was previously addressed in the Buildings chapter.

After "Butcher" Benton (Lon Chaney, Jr.) escapes from an experimental laboratory near San Francisco, he comes to Los Angeles to get revenge on the man who sent him to prison.

Chaney comes to the intersection of 3rd and Hill streets and climbs a cement stairway to the top of Bunker Hill. The old Angel's Flight is seen throughout this lengthy film segment.

« *Tell Me No Secrets* »

One of the first motion pictures filmed at the new Angel's Flight, this 1997 release stars Lori Loughlin as a district attorney stalked and psychologically terrorized by a rapist she unsuccessfully prosecuted.

In one lengthy scene, Loughlin leaves her office and takes Angel's Flight to the top of Bunker Hill en route to a garage where her car is parked.

The old Angel's Flight location is on the south side of the 3rd Street Tunnel at the intersection of 3rd and Hill streets. Map Code: 634 F4.

The new Angel's Flight location is one block south of the original site, on Hill Street near 4th Street.

SANTA ANITA DEPOT (ARCADIA)

The Arboretum of Los Angeles County was previously addressed in the Houses and the Lakes chapters of this book. Within this complex is the Santa Anita Depot, a railroad station located just south of the Queen Anne Cottage.

This railroad depot is a location in segments of the following motion picture and television series.

« *Christmas in Connecticut* »

Covered with fake snow and said to be in Connecticut, the depot is the backdrop for scenes in this 1992 television remake of the 1945 classic film of the same title that starred Barbara Stanwyck and Dennis Morgan. This movie stars Dyan Cannon and Kris Kristofferson in the lead roles.

The majority of filming was done at the Grand Teton National Park in Wyoming, also with fake snow.

The Arboretum of Los Angeles County's Santa Anita Depot, a location for the 1992 motion picture *Christmas in Connecticut* and for segments of the television series *Scene of the Crime*. (Photograph taken in 1986.)

« *Scene of the Crime* » *(1985)*

Orson Welles is the host of this mystery television series, and the Santa Anita Depot is a location in one segment starring Michelle Phillips.

The Arboretum of Los Angeles County is located at 301 North Baldwin Avenue, in Arcadia, California, south of the Foothill Freeway (210). Map Code: 567 A5.

PASADENA TRAIN STATION (PASADENA)

The Pasadena Train Station (Depot) closed in 1994 because Amtrak rerouted its Continental Southwest Chief through Orange County. Plans are being made to convert the station to service passengers of a future commuter rail line, however.

For the past 108 years this location has served the community with the legendary trains the California Limited, the Super Chief, the El Capitan and the Grand Canyon Limited, all of which stopped on a regular basis.

The third depot constructed on this site, this Spanish-style building, only 10 miles from downtown Los Angeles, was a favorite arrival and departure location in the 1930s and 1940s for celebrities such as Clark Gable, Mae West, Will Rogers, Gary Cooper, Jeanette MacDonald, Errol

The Pasadena Train Station, near Del Mar Boulevard and Arroyo Parkway in Pasadena, California. (Photograph taken in 1986.)

Flynn and, of course, Jean Harlow, simply to avoid the press and overzealous fans.

Segments of the following motion pictures were filmed at this location, all showing arrivals or departures from a train.

« Star Dust »

The plot of this 1940 motion picture will be addressed later in this chapter.

« Harlow »

Carroll Baker is legendary movie star Jean Harlow in this 1965 motion picture. This film follows her brief life in Los Angeles and Hollywood to her tragic death on June 7, 1937, at the age of 26 of uremic poison.

The Pasadena Train Station is located near the intersection of Del Mar Boulevard and Arroyo Parkway in Pasadena, California. Map Code: 565 H5.

SANTA FE RAILROAD STATION (LOS ANGELES)

The Santa Fe Railroad Station served the greater Los Angeles area as a major transportation complex until the nearby Union Station opened on May 3, 1939. (The latter will be addressed later in this chapter).

The Santa Fe Railroad Station was demolished in the 1950s, and the site is now occupied by the Light Rail-Metro Rail Maintenance Facility.

The following motion pictures were filmed, in part, at this location, all with the station building in the scenes.

« Blue of the Night »

Bing Crosby and Babe Kane board "Train Number 20, the Chief," at this station en route to New York from Los Angeles in this 1932 Mack Sennett short film.

RAILROAD STATIONS 185

The site of the old Santa Fe Railroad Station, now a maintenance facility, looking south from the 1st Street Viaduct. (Photograph taken in 1998.)

Never meeting Crosby, but in love with him from his radio voice, Kane tells the man seated next to her that she is engaged to Crosby, unaware she is talking to the famous crooner.

Crosby plays along all the way to New York, where Kane's boyfriend (Franklin Pangborn) refuses to believe Crosby is actually Crosby, which results in a bet wherein the singer wins Pangborn's new Cadillac convertible by singing "Blue of the Night."

« Lady Killer »

The plot of this 1933 film was previously addressed in the Airports chapter of this book.

James Cagney, fleeing New York City with a female member (Mae Clarke) of the gang he is involved with, boards a train, the "California Limited," en route to Los Angeles.

The boarding location east of the site of the old Santa Fe Railroad Station, now a small maintenance building, looking south from the 1st Street Viaduct. (Photograph taken in 1998.)

The train arrives in Los Angeles at this railroad station. As soon as Cagney and Clarke leave the train and enter the station, Cagney is confronted by police detectives and taken away for interrogation relating to his gang association in New York City.

« Show Them No Mercy »

The plot of this 1935 motion picture centers on a young couple (Rochelle Hudson and Edward Norris) who come to an old house that turns out to be the hideout of a gang of criminals.
The railroad station and the adjoining railroad yards are seen as one of the criminals (Warren Hymer) is shot as he attempts to escape by boarding a train for Phoenix, Arizona.

« Blondie Plays Cupid »

In this 1940 release, the seventh entry of the 28-film series, Blondie (Penny Singleton) and Dagwood (Arthur Lake) stumble and fumble their way through the typical Bumstead plot.

Near the opening of this film, Blondie and Dagwood decide to go visit an aunt by train. In a lengthy scene at this location, a scene that has an outstanding view of the station and the adjoining railroad yards, Dagwood boards the wrong train, then chases the train Blondie is on, finally catching it as it exits the railroad yards.

The Santa Fe Railroad Station is also a part of Hollywood and Los Angeles history since it is the location of the train carrying the body of the screen legend Rudolph Valentino arrived in from New York City in 1926. The hearse led a procession of automobiles carrying many of the motion picture industry through the streets of Los Angeles to Hollywood Memorial Park Cemetery where Valentino was interred.

The site of the Santa Fe Railroad Station is 284 S. Santa Fe Avenue, south of the 1st Street Viaduct in downtown Los Angeles. Map Code: 634 H4.

UNION STATION (LOS ANGELES)

The Union Station (The Union Passenger Terminal) replaced the Santa Fe Railroad Station when the former officially opened on May 3, 1939. This magnificent Spanish Mission–style facility was constructed at a cost of $11 million and took over five years to complete. It proved to be the last large railroad passenger terminal built in the United States. It is Historic-Cultural Monument #101.

Segments of the following motion pictures and television series were filmed at this location, all showing arrivals or departures.

« Star Dust »

This 1940 motion picture, a typical Hollywood success story, focuses on a Hollywood talent scout (Roland Young) who discovers two young people (Linda Darnell and John Payne) and helps them climb that difficult ladder to stardom.

« *Bugsy* »

The plot of this 1991 movie was previously addressed in the City Halls chapter of this book.

« *Sinatra* »

This 1992 television movie focuses on legendary Frank Sinatra's (Phillip Casnoff) career from his Hoboken, New Jersey, start in a lengthy singing career to his later mob connections and his friendship with the Kennedys.

« *The Invaders* »

The plot of this 1995 sci-fi film was previously addressed in the Bridges chapter.

« *Species* »

The plot of this 1995 sci-fi thriller was previously addressed in the Piers chapter of this book.
In one lengthy scene, the half-human, half-alien (Natasha Henstridge) arrives in Los Angeles at this station as a grown woman after leaving Dugway, Utah, the day before as a young girl.

« *Once You Meet a Stranger* »

The plot of this 1996 motion picture was previously addressed in the Police Stations chapter.

Opposite: **The Union Station, located at 800 N. Alameda Street in downtown Los Angeles, a very popular film location. (Photograph taken in 1998.)**

RAILROAD STATIONS

The loading/unloading area of the Union Station. (Photograph taken in 1998.)

« *The Jack Benny Program* » *(1950–1965)*

Radio and motion picture comedian Jack Benny easily makes the jump to television with a weekly comedy show that features guests and skits performed by his company of regulars, including Benny's wife, Mary Livingston, Eddie Anderson (Rochester) and announcer Don Wilson.

« *Profiler* » *(1996–)*

In this television series, Dr. Sam Waters (Ally Walker), a psychic, is teamed with Robert Davi and others who travel about to the scenes of crimes to investigate and assist the local detectives in apprehending those responsible.

« Shell Game »
(1987)

A divorced couple and former con artists (James Read and Margot Kidder) get back together to produce a consumer affairs television show in Santa Ana, California, in this short-lived television series.

The Union Station is located at 800 N. Alameda Street, north of the Hollywood Freeway (101) in downtown Los Angeles. Map Code: 634 G3.

The railroad station located in the Universal Studios complex was fully addressed in the Movie Studios chapter of this book. Please refer to that chapter for information on this station.

Ranches

Corrigan Ranch (Simi Valley)
Iverson Ranch (Simi Valley)
Melody Ranch (Newhall)
Placerita Canyon State Park (Newhall)

When the fledgling motion picture industry finally settled in Hollywood, California, in the early part of the 20th century, that district of the city of Los Angeles was a remote suburb with hundreds of acres of open spaces, hills and foothills that quickly and regularly served as locations for segments of motion pictures that could not be filmed on studio back lots.

As the city of Los Angeles rapidly grew in the 1920s, it surrounded and eventually engulfed Hollywood with scores of housing developments, virtually eliminating nearby locations for motion picture filming.

This lack of space necessitated a move that most motion picture studios grudgingly but gradually accepted, and most either bought property miles away from Hollywood or rented available property that enterprising businessmen offered at a reasonable price. Thus were born movie ranches, many of which still exist today, serving motion picture and television series production companies.

The following movie ranches have served as locations for segments of the many listed motion picture and television series productions.

Corrigan Ranch (Simi Valley)

The Corrigan Ranch property in Simi Valley, California, was purchased in 1938 by Western movie star Ray "Crash" Corrigan of the "Three Mesquiteers" motion picture series fame who named the ranch "Corriganville," He first used the property as a film location in 1940 when he started the "Range Busters" Western motion picture series.

Movie legend Bob Hope later owned the ranch and at that time it was known as "Hopetown" and "Hopeville." Now, plans are being made to keep the majority of ranch property free from a rapidly approaching housing development and convert it into a park.

The majority of segments filmed here were shot east of the entrance in a large oak forest that contains a cement-lined lake with a below-the-surface location, complete with a large glass window for underwater filming, and a man-made cement cliff hovering above the north bank of the lake that allowed buckboards and stagecoaches to roll off of it and into the water at the end of a thrilling chase scene.

Immediately north of the lake are a series of trails where many stagecoaches, buckboards and horses carried their heroes and villains to or from a hectic encounter.

« Fort Apache »

R.K.O. Radio Pictures contracted the outstanding team of John Ford (director) and John Wayne (actor) to address a plot revolving around an Indian uprising that threatens a U.S. Army fort in the Wild West.

Ford actually had a fort constructed on the ranch to serve as a principal location throughout this 1948 western.

« Jungle Jim »

Based on Alex Raymond's comic-strip hero, this 1948 motion picture, the first in the 16-feature film series, finds the lead character, portrayed by the former Tarzan, Johnny Weissmuller, taking a scientist (Virginia Grey) on a search in a dense jungle to locate a witch doctor who possesses a miracle drug.

The cliff and the lake are sites where the group camped and where Weissmuller dove into the lake to rescue Grey, who was attacked by an alligator as she took a swim before retiring.

« *The Three Musketeers* »

Alexandre Dumas' novel comes to life in the third talking motion picture version (the previous two releases were in 1935 and in 1939). A great cast includes Lana Turner, June Allyson and Gene Kelly, who cavort their way through this swashbuckling tale with lots of swordfights.

The forest in the ranch and the lake are in several scenes in this 1948 adventure.

« *The Baron of Arizona* »

A fact-based drama, this 1950 motion picture stars Vincent Price as a conniving man who nearly becomes the Baron of Arizona in the 19th century.

A Western street near the entrance to the ranch is a primary location in the film.

« *Vendetta* »

The Western street of the ranch is a primary location in this 1950 costume drama that stars Faith Domergue and Nigel Bruce in a plot revolving around a woman (Domergue) attempting to avenge the death of her father.

The forest on the ranch is also a location in the film.

« *Jungle Jim* » *(1955)*

Johnny Weissmuller of "Tarzan" fame appears as a guide in Africa in this abbreviated television series.

The lake and the forest are frequent locations.

Opposite: **The oak tree forest in Corrigan Ranch in Simi, California, the location of many films, especially Westerns. (Photograph taken in 1986.)**

The lake (now dry) and the artificial cliff in Corrigan Ranch. (Photograph taken in 1986.)

« Rin Tin Tin » *(1954-1959)*

Television's most popular German shepherd is the star of this series. Set in the Old West at the fort of the 101st Cavalry, Lee Aaker is Rin Tin Tin's master, Rusty, and Jim Brown is Lt. Ripley "Rip" Masters, the leader of the 101st.

All 164 episodes of the series were filmed on this ranch.

The Corrigan Ranch is located on Kuehner Drive at Smith Road, south of the Simi Valley Freeway (118)* in Simi Valley, California. Map Code: 499 C3 & D3.

Also called the Ronald Reagan Freeway.

Iverson Ranch (Simi Valley)

One of the most-photographed locations in Hollywood motion picture history, the Iverson Ranch was the site of the filming of more than 2,000 motion pictures, television series and serial segments, beginning in 1912.

The sprawling 600-acre ranch area, owned by the Iverson family, consisted of two areas, the Upper Iverson and the Lower Iverson, now split by the Simi Valley Freeway (118). The Upper Iverson, with the beautiful Santa Susana Mountains as a background, was the location for countless Western scenes, primarily chases. The Lower Iverson, more hilly and rugged, with boulders of all shapes and sizes scattered about, was the location for motion pictures, television series and serials requiring that type of setting.

A centerpiece of Lower Iverson is a huge boulder that is known to many motion picture buffs as "Indian Head Rock."

Nearby is the famous "Arch Rock," a popular location for prehistoric-type motion pictures, Westerns and serials.

Progress has taken its toll on this ranch, however, as a private residential community has engulfed the majority of the Lower Iverson, but the contractor was careful to preserve the basic landscape and much of the rock formations, keeping as much of Hollywood motion picture history intact as possible.

Author Robert G. Sherman's book *Quiet on the Set* eloquently covers the history of the Iverson Ranch, beginning with the first film shot there in 1912. Included are photographs of scores of films taken at the time of production.

The following major motion pictures, television series and serials were, in part, filmed at this ranch.

« *The Three Ages* »

This 1923 silent motion picture stars comedian Buster Keaton working his way through three love stories, opening with "Stone Age," moving to "Roman Age" and concluding with "Modern Age."

The "Arch Rock" formation is a primary location in the "Stone Age" segment of this film.

« The Gold Rush »

A timeless classic, this 1925 silent features Charlie Chaplin en route to the Yukon Territory of Alaska in search of gold. Several scenes were shot on the ranch.

The film was reedited and rereleased decades later with a music score and narration by Chaplin.

« Ben-Hur »

Ramon Novarro is the star of this 1926 silent motion picture that relates the story of a galley-slave interwoven with the historic events leading to the death of Jesus Christ.

This film was remade in 1959 with Charlton Heston in the starring role.

The spectacular chariot races in both film versions were shot on the grounds of the ranch.

« Hell's Angels »

The motion picture that launched sexy Jean Harlow to stardom, this 1930 Howard Hughes production centers on fliers attempting to survive World War I in flimsy airplanes. Aside from Harlow's performance, this film boasts a Technicolor party sequence and tinted action at night.

Many airplane crash scenes were filmed at the ranch.

« The Lives of a Bengal Lancer »

The rolling hills and boulders of all sizes provide the perfect Northwest India setting for this 1935 motion picture starring Gary Cooper and Franchot Tone as members of the famous British regiment. The story is based on the novel by Major Francis Yeats-Brown.

« The Trail of the Lonesome Pine »

The original, a silent movie about families who feud when a railroad crosses their land, was released in 1915. This 1936 film follows the same plot and is recorded as the first motion picture filmed on location in full Technicolor. Henry Fonda and Sylvia Sidney star.

« *The Adventures of Marco Polo* »

The famous explorer's trips from Italy to China are the centerpiece of this 1938 motion picture starring Gary Cooper as Marco Polo and Basil Rathbone in his early film characterization as the ultimate villain. Screen legend Lana Turner has a bit part in the film.

The ranch landscape serves as the area of China where Marco Polo originally met and lived with the Chinese.

« *Wee Willie Winkie* »

Shirley Temple is at her best in this 1937 motion picture set at a British outpost in remote India. Temple is befriended by an army sergeant (Victor McLaglen) and loved by her grandfather (C. Aubrey Smith), who is the colonel in charge of the outpost. Eventually, Shirley is instrumental in settling a festering dispute between the army and Indian natives led by Cesar Romero.

Romero's headquarters is located in the ranch's rocks near Indian Head Rock, and the army outpost is located nearby.

« *The Good Earth* »

The rolling hills of the ranch are once again rural China in this 1937 motion picture based on the novel by author Pearl Buck that relates the story of a poor Chinese couple barely existing on their plot of land. Paul Muni and Luise Rainer star.

« *The Oklahoma Kid* »

This classic Western motion picture, filmed in 1939, features James Cagney as a cowboy out to revenge the unlawful lynching of his father. Humphrey Bogart, dressed in black garb, is the perfect villain.

All location shooting in this film is at the ranch.

The famous "Indian Head Rock" at the Iverson Ranch, a location in scores of motion pictures. (Photograph taken in 1986.)

« One Night in the Tropics »

Significant as the film debut of comedians Bud Abbott and Lou Costello, this 1940 musical is based on a love triangle involving Allan Jones, Nancy Kelly and Robert Cummings.

Only a few scenes of the film were shot at the ranch.

« One Million B.C. »

A vast section of the ranch needed props to make the landscape appear prehistoric in this 1939 motion picture that stars Victor Mature and Carole Landis.

The plot is told in flashback. Outstanding special effects include prehistoric monsters and a horrendous volcano eruption.

« *They Died with Their Boots On* »

Errol Flynn portrays the legendary and flamboyant George Armstrong Custer from his days as a cadet at West Point to the Little Big Horn River and his historic Last Stand in this 1941 motion picture.

In one memorable scene filmed at the ranch, Flynn rides his horse to meet Chief Crazy Horse (Anthony Quinn) prior to the great battle. They meet and talk in front of Indian Head Rock.

This film proved to be the last appearance of Errol Flynn and Olivia de Havilland as costars.

« *Sahara* »

A World War II entry, this 1943 motion picture pits a stranded British-American military unit against a German Army unit in the desolate Sahara Desert in North Africa. With tons of sand added, a part of the ranch serves as that famous desert. Humphrey Bogart stars as a tank sergeant.

« *The Treasure of the Sierra Madre* »

Now a section of Mexico, the ranch is the location where three prospectors (Humphrey Bogart, Walter Huston and Tim Holt) strike it rich at a gold mine in this 1948 film.

« *Elephant Walk* »

A hilly area of the ranch became a tea planation in the jungles of Ceylon in this 1954 drama that stars Elizabeth Taylor and Dana Andrews. The film climaxes with the total destruction of the plantation by a herd of elephants and a fire.

« *A Face in the Crowd* »

A part of the ranch is the location of a rural Southern community in this 1957 movie, the plot of which centers on a homespun drifter (Andy

Griffith) discovered by Patricia Neal and turned into an extremely successful television star. Griffith and Lee Remick make their debuts.

« Annie Oakley » (1952–1956)

The ranch provides the setting for the Western town of Diablo in this television series that was the first to star a woman. Gail Davis played the legendary sharpshooter.

« The Cisco Kid » (1950–1955)

First appearing on radio in 1943, this "Robin Hood of the West" hero was a natural for a television series in the early days of that medium. Duncan Renaldo stars as the Kid, and Leo Carillo appears as Pancho, the Kid's sidekick.

The duo are hunted as criminals across the ranch by lawmen, but are loved for helping the poor and others in need of their assistance.

« Hopalong Cassidy » (1949–1954)

The Upper Iverson area is the location of many chase scenes in this television series that stars William Boyd—an actor who *was* Hopalong Cassidy to generations of moviegoers, as he starred in 66 Hopalong Cassidy motion pictures from 1935 to 1948.

« The Roy Rogers Show » (1951–1957)

A Western television series that takes place in present-day, *The Roy Rogers Show* was shot at the ranch and was a popular vehicle for Western motion picture stars Roy Rogers and his wife, Dale Evans. The series lasted for 101 episodes.

"Arch Rock" at Iverson Ranch, seen in many motion pictures. (Photograph taken in 1986.)

« Undersea Kingdom »

This 12-chapter serial, released in 1936, stars Ray "Crash" Corrigan as the hero who accompanies Professor Norton (C. Montague Shaw) under the ocean to the lost continent of Atlantis to investigate the cause of a series of severe earthquakes shaking North America.

The ranch is a primary location for scenes both above and below the surface of the ocean.

« Zorro Rides Again »

Zorro (John Carroll) rides all over the ranch and survives 12 chapters in this 1937 serial as he vows to avenge the death of his uncle (Nigel de Brulier) and stop a villain (Noah Beery) from gaining control of a railroad company.

« The Lone Ranger »

The ranch is the Old West in this classic serial, a 15-chapter 1938 thriller that stars Lee Powell as the Lone Ranger and Chief Thunder Cloud as Tonto. The two heroes ride the trails of the West in the years following the Civil War to bring law and order to communities where none exist.

As mentioned earlier, the ranch is bisected by the Simi Valley Freeway (118). To reach the original entrance to the ranch, exit the freeway at Topanga Canyon Boulevard. Go south a short distance to the first intersection, Santa Susana Pass Road. Turn right (west) and go approximately one mile to the entrance to the ranch, now the entrance to a housing development. Map Code: 499 J2.

MELODY RANCH (NEWHALL)

Fans of Westerns immediately associate Gene Autry with Melody Ranch, as it was used by Autry as a location for many of his films and loaned to other motion picture studios for location filming.

Segments of the following motion pictures and television series were filmed on ranch property, primarily near the entrance on the main street.

« Riders of Destiny »

John Wayne, a government agent, poses as a wanted man to obtain evidence on a man attempting to get settlers to sell their land at a low price by cutting off their water supply in this 1933 film.

« Tumbling Tumbleweeds »

Gene Autry and Smiley Burnette star in this 1935 motion picture, Autry's first feature film. Autry, a medicine show performer, attempts to find the killer of his father to clear a friend falsely accused of the crime.

Main Street at Melody Ranch in Newhall, California, the location of many Western films and the site of Laurel and Hardy's dance scene in *Way Out West*, their popular 1937 film. (Photograph taken in 1986.)

« Way Out West »

In this 1937 comedy, the 90th film and the 57th "talkie" Laurel and Hardy made together, the duo arrives in Brushwood Gulch to deliver a deed to a gold mine to Mary Roberts (Rosina Lawrence), the only child of the deceased owner of the mine. Lawrence is employed at Mickey Finn's Saloon, owned by Finn (James Finlayson), who causes Laurel and Hardy nothing but trouble throughout the film.

In one scene early in the film, Laurel and Hardy stop outside the saloon to enjoy a song, "At the Ball, That's All," being sung by the Avalon Boys Quartet (a later Western film star, Chill Wills, is a member of the quartet), then soon begin a dance familiar to all Laurel and Hardy fans and motion picture historians.

« Mexicali Rose »

It's Gene Autry and Smiley Burnette again in 1939, this time out to stop an oil discovery scam a bunch of crooks are trying to sell to townspeople.

« The Virginian »

Based on author Owen Wister's novel published in 1902, this 1946 Western is the fourth version to appear on the silver screen. Joel McCrea stars as a cowboy who loses the love of his girl when he is forced to hang his friend after the friend is caught rustling cattle.

« The Big Sombrero »

Noted for being one of the first Western motion pictures in color, this 1949 release has Gene Autry doing his best to stop a crook from marrying a rich girl (Elena Verdugo) to gain control of her ranch so he can sell it for an enormous profit.

« Tombstone Territory » (1957–1959)

This half-hour television series stars Pat Conway as Sheriff Clay Hollister and Richard Eastham as Harris Claibourne, the editor of the *Tombstone Epitaph*, the town's only newspaper. Conway gets in and out of scrape after scrape, and Eastham prints it in his newspaper office located on the main street of the ranch.

« Wyatt Earp » (1955–1961)

The Life and Legend of Wyatt Earp is the actual title of this television series, but it is more commonly known by the shorter title.

The series is loosely based on the life of the legendary Western lawman Wyatt Earp (Hugh O'Brien), who is the marshall of Dodge City, Kansas, during the first four seasons of the series. Later, Earp is the marshall of Tombstone, Arizona. The main street of the ranch serves as a location for both Kansas and Arizona.

Melody Ranch is located on Oak Creek Avenue at Placeritos Boulevard, north of Placerita Canyon Road and west of the Antelope Valley Freeway (14) in Newhall, California. Map Code: 4641 B1.

PLACERITA CANYON STATE PARK (NEWHALL)

Placerita Canyon, the eponym of Placerita Canyon State Park, was formerly known as Walker Ranch, the location for hundreds of motion pictures, primarily Westerns, and television series productions.

The centerpiece of the park today is a log cabin near the parking area just inside the park's entrance. Now shaded by a magnificent sycamore tree, the cabin, built in 1920 by ranch owner Frank Walker for his wife and 12 children, was seen in many Western motion pictures in the 1930s. Today it is a starting point to begin a trek into the canyon and to locations familiar to fans worldwide.

The following motion picture was filmed, in part, at this ranch.

« Way Out West »

This 1937 Laurel and Hardy motion picture was previously addressed in the Iverson Ranch section of this chapter.

The ranch is the location of the opening and closing scenes of this comedy. Laurel and Hardy, en route to Brushwood Gulch, cross a stream that Hardy falls into; then, upon their return trip with Mary Roberts (Rosina Lawrence) astride a mule (Dinah), Hardy again falls into the water.

The location of these two scenes is east of the parking area at a stream near the Los Pineots Trail.

208   RANCHES

The trail leading into Placerita Canyon State Park in Newhall, California, where many films were shot, including the scene in Laurel and Hardy's 1937 film *Way Out West* where Oliver Hardy fell into a stream several times. (Photograph taken in 1989.)

The Placerita Canyon State Park is located on Placerita Canyon Road, 1¼ miles east of the Antelope Valley Freeway (14) and north of the Golden State Freeway (5) near the city of Newhall, California. Map Code: 4641 G1.

Reservoirs

Hollywood Reservoir (Hollywood)

Like the majority of communities across the United States, the greater Los Angeles area is sprinkled with an assortment of dams and reservoirs to provide water for normal household use and for the giant agricultural industry in the county.

HOLLYWOOD RESERVOIR (HOLLYWOOD)

The Hollywood Reservoir, dedicated in 1925, is part of a vast network of waterways that serves the Hollywood area of the city of Los Angeles, providing water for over 500,000 persons daily.
Segments of the following motion pictures were filmed at this location.

« *Quicksand: No Escape* »

Donald Sutherland stars as a private detective and blackmailer who is hired by the wife (Felicity Huffman) of an architect (Tim Matheson) she

A frequent film location, the Hollywood Reservoir is located near Lake Hollywood Drive in Hollywood. (Photograph taken in 1987.)

suspects of having an affair. Instead of doing the investigation, Sutherland frames Matheson for the murder of a vice-cop in this 1991 television movie.

This reservoir is the location of a meeting between Sutherland and Matheson.

« Rescue Me »

The plot of this 1993 motion picture was previously addressed in the Piers chapter of this book.

This reservoir is the location of a meeting between the kidnappers and representatives of the cheerleader's family for a ransom payoff that results in a shoot-out.

The Hollywood Reservoir is located in the Hollywood District of the city of Los Angeles and can be reached from two different directions.

From a location east of the Hollywood Freeway (101), it can be approached east of Barham Boulevard at the terminus of Lake Hollywood Drive. Map Code: 593 E1.

From a location north of the Hollywood Freeway, it can be approached north of Franklin Avenue and east of Cahuenga Boulevard, at the end of Weidlake Drive. Map Code: 593 F2.

As a note of interest, construction of this reservoir began in 1923 and was completed in 1924. It is a part of a massive waterway project begun in 1908, bringing water 250 miles from the Owens River Valley in Central California.

The reservoir formed Hollywood Lake. It is 200 feet high and 160 feet thick at its base, and was dedicated on March 17, 1925, as Mulholland Dam, named after the engineer responsible for bringing water to the city of Los Angeles, William Mulholland. It was renamed the Hollywood Reservoir shortly after the St. Francis Dam disaster in Sagus, California, on March 12–13, 1928, which claimed 400 lives. The disaster was blamed on Mulholland, who had personally inspected the dam hours earlier and declared it safe.

Rivers

Los Angeles River (Los Angeles)

LOS ANGELES RIVER (LOS ANGELES)

Certainly a river during the rainy California winters as it carries a vast amount of water from the distant foothills through the heart of the city to the Pacific Ocean, the Los Angeles River reverts to a mere stream during the dry months of each year.

With angled cement embankments and a cement bed and channel, this river, over the years, has served as a location for motion picture and television series production companies.

Segments of the following productions were filmed at this river.

« *The Annihilator* »

The plot of this 1986 thriller will be addressed in the Tunnels chapter of this book.

The riverbed is the location of a chase scene between the 4th Street and 6th Street viaducts.

The Los Angeles River, looking south from the 1st Street Viaduct toward the 4th Street Viaduct. (Photograph taken in 1998.)

« *Condor* »

The riverbed between the 4th Street and 6th Street viaducts is the location of a chase between futuristic cars near the end of this 1986 film, which is set in the city of Los Angeles in 1999.

« *Wedlock* »

The plot of this 1991 motion picture takes place "sometime in the future" in Los Angeles and stars Rutger Hauer as a jewel thief arrested and incarcerated in a high-tech prison where inmates are fitted with a metal collar set to explode should they attempt escape.

As the film begins, Hauer is pursued by police into the *Them!* Tunnel and this river, where he escapes into a storm drain and eventually surfaces through a manhole in the middle of Santa Fe Avenue near the 6th Street Viaduct.

All locations in this chapter are found in Map Code: 634 H4 & H5.

Roads

Santa Susana Pass Road (Simi Valley)

SANTA SUSANA PASS ROAD (SIMI VALLEY)

If one road could be selected as the most familiar to motion picture fans worldwide, it would be the Santa Susana Pass Road, a two-lane thoroughfare that twists and turns from Topanga Canyon Boulevard in the Chatsworth District of the city of Los Angeles to its terminus several miles west where it becomes Kuehner Drive in the Ventura County community of Simi Valley, near the old Corriganville Movie Ranch (discussed in the Ranches chapter).

Slightly west of Topanga Canyon Boulevard, this road crosses over a historic railroad tunnel that will be addressed in the Tunnels chapter, and a mile farther west is the Iverson Movie Ranch (addressed in the Ranches chapter).

Aside from these historic motion picture locations, however, this road is familiar because of the countless vehicle chase scenes filmed on it in scores of movies during the 1930s and the 1940s.

Car chasing a car, car chasing a truck, truck chasing a car, motorcycle chasing both—any vehicle chase one can imagine was filmed on this road.

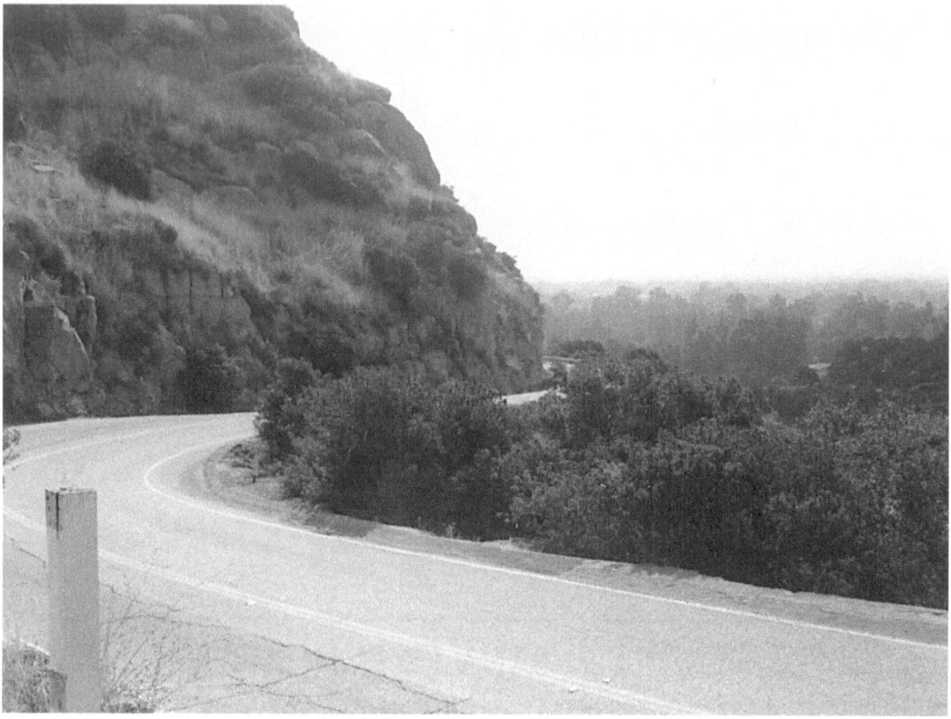

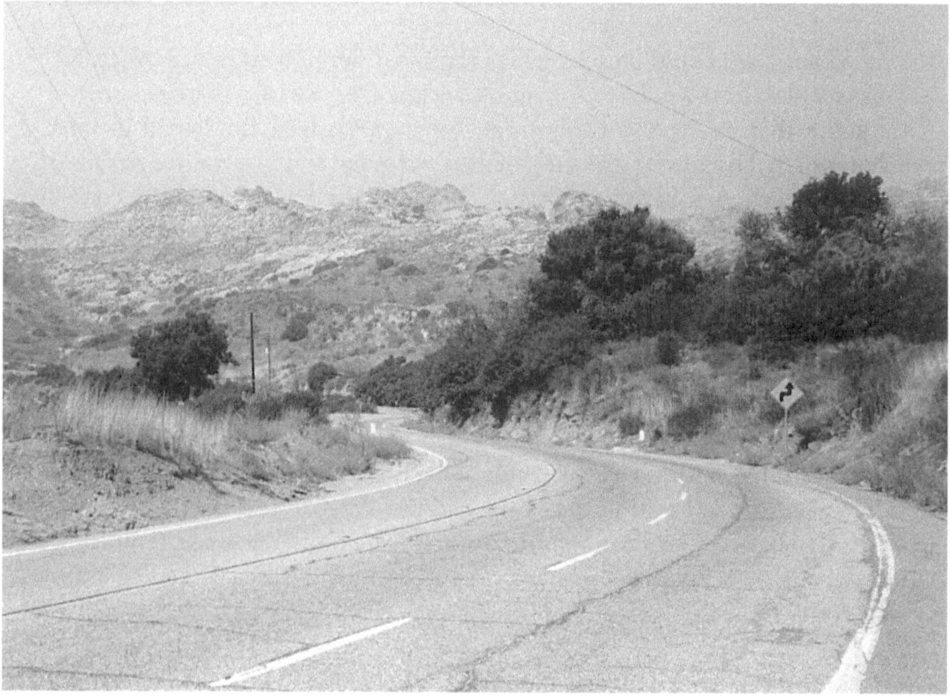

Even car wrecks, explosions and over-the-cliff segments of motion pictures and serials were regularly filmed at this location.

A slow drive along this road, regardless of where one begins or ends, is a nostalgic venture through motion picture history. It is found south of the Simi Valley Freeway (118). The road begins at Map Code: 500 A3 and ends at Map Code: 499 C4.

Opposite Top: The Santa Susana Pass Road, looking east from the Iverson Ranch toward Los Angeles. (Photograph taken in 1986.)

Opposite Bottom: The Santa Susana Pass Road, twisting west from the Iverson Ranch toward Corrigan Ranch in Simi Valley. (Photograph taken in 1986.)

Schools

Beverly Hills High School (Beverly Hills)
Los Angeles Valley College (Van Nuys)
Marshall High School (Los Angeles)
M-G-M School (Culver City)
Whittier High School (Whittier)

A variety of Los Angeles area schools have been and continue to be locations for segments of motion picture and television series production companies.

Permission must be gained for such filming, done primarily during the summer months of the year when the majority of the students are on summer break.

Generally, the schools selected by production companies are the ones constructed in the 1920s and the 1930s because of the more ornate architecture, a style not present on today's school buildings.

A prime example is the high school featured in the television series *Beverly Hills 90210*. Torrance High School, a school located many miles south of Beverly Hills in the city of Torrance, was chosen as West Beverly High by the production company because of its Gothic architecture.

Beverly Hills High School (Beverly Hills)

Beverly Hills High School, located in the 5.6 square mile affluent community of Beverly Hills, California, has the reputation of having a student body consisting mainly of children of Hollywood stars and of graduating many of the major motion picture and television personalities of the past and present since 1928.

The school's gymnasium is unique as it has a wooden floor that opens hydraulically to reveal a 50' × 75' swimming pool, which was prominent in a lengthy scene in the 1946 motion picture classic *It's a Wonderful Life*.

This facility was the subject of worldwide interest in January 1998, when it was revealed that Monica Lewinsky, who was at that time embroiled in a controversy relating to an alleged sexual encounter with President Clinton, was also allegedly involved in a five-year sexual affair with Andy Bleller, a former drama instructor she met here when she was a student.

The high school complex is a location in segments of the following motion pictures.

« *The Bachelor and the Bobby-Soxer* »

Cary Grant stars as a playboy who is "sentenced" by a judge (Myrna Loy) to discourage her kid sister's (Shirley Temple) crush on him. Loy eventually falls for Grant.

In this 1947 romantic comedy, Temple attends this high school and in one lengthy scene takes Grant to the gymnasium to watch a school basketball game.

« *Tagget* »

In this 1991 movie, Daniel J. Travanti stars as a disabled Vietnam veteran determined to find out the truth about a secret mission that ends in a massacre during that conflict.

The high school is the location of a secret meeting Travanti has with a person willing to help him.

The interior of the Beverly Hills High School gymnasium, seen in *It's a Wonderful Life* (1946) and *The Bachelor and the Bobby-Soxer* (1947). (Photograph taken in 1988.)

Beverly Hills High School is located at 241 South Moreno Drive, south of Santa Monica Boulevard and east of the San Diego Freeway (405).

The gymnasium is located south of the main school building, next to the athletic field at the intersection of Lasky Drive and Moreno Drive.

Both locations are in Map Code: 623 E3.

Opposite: Beverly Hills High School, located at 241 S. Moreno Drive, Beverly Hills. (Photograph taken in 1988.)

LOS ANGELES VALLEY COLLEGE
(VAN NUYS)

Los Angeles Valley College in Van Nuys, California, with its campus dotted with a wide variety of trees, served as a location for segments of the following motion picture.

« *Throw Momma from the Train* »

In a 1987 spinoff of Alfred Hitchcock's 1951 film *Strangers on a Train*, Danny DeVito attempts to persuade his writing professor (Billy Crystal) to murder DeVito's nagging mother (Anne Ramsey) in exchange for the

The Los Angeles Valley College campus, in Van Nuys, seen in *Throw Momma from the Train* (1987). (Photograph taken in 1989.)

determined pupil's carrying out the murder of Crystal's wife (Kate Mulgrew).

The college is a location in the scene wherein DeVito first meets Crystal in the writing class.

The Los Angeles Valley College is located at 5800 Fulton Avenue in Van Nuys, north of the Ventura Freeway (101) and east of the San Diego Freeway (405). Map Code: 562 D1.

MARSHALL HIGH SCHOOL (LOS ANGELES)

Marshall High School is not only a very popular location for production companies but is famous worldwide as the building located behind the original Walt Disney Studios in the Silverlake District of Los Angeles and can be seen in the background of vintage photographs taken of the Walt Disney Studios.

Segments of the following motion pictures and television series productions were filmed at this high school.

« Zapped »

Scott Baio, a science whiz whose screwball experiment allows him to see through the clothing of fellow students, attends this high school in this 1982 motion picture.

« Nightmare »

The high school is in one scene in this 1991 movie starring Victoria Principal as a single parent struggling to get justice for her 11-year-old child who was molested.

« Midnight's Child »

The plot of this 1992 motion picture centers on a housekeeper who has an insight into the supernatural. Marcy Walker and Olivia D'Abo star.

224   SCHOOLS

Marshall High School, situated at 3101 Griffith Park Boulevard, Los Angeles. (Photograph taken in 1997.)

The high school is the St. Helena Academy, a European Catholic convent and school in the film.

« In the Shadows, Someone's Watching »

This 1993 psychological drama motion picture takes place in the small town of Tyler Grove, where preteens are stalked.

The high school serves as the Tyler Grove Hospital in this film, which is based on the novel of the same title by Judith Kelman and stars Joan Van Ark.

Opposite: The M-G-M school building, located on studio property at 10202 W. Washington Boulevard, Culver City. (Photograph taken in 1984.)

SCHOOLS 225

« *True Crime* »

Alicia Silverstone is an amateur sleuth who teams with a police cadet (Kevin Dillon) and tries to catch a serial killer preying on teenage girls in this 1996 motion picture.

This high school serves as the school attended by Silverstone in this film.

Marshall High School is located at 3101 Griffith Park Boulevard, Los Angeles, California, west of the Golden State Freeway (5). Map Code: 594 C3.

M-G-M SCHOOL (CULVER CITY)

The M-G-M School, a small stucco building with a Spanish-style, red tile roof, is almost lost between huge sound stages on the M-G-M Studios back lot. Now containing offices for a production company, this

building once served as a school for many of the young actors under contract to the studio, including Elizabeth Taylor and many of the kids who appeared in the Our Gang film series.

The M-G-M Studio complex is located at 10202 West Washington Boulevard in Culver City, California, south of the Santa Monica Freeway (10).

WHITTIER HIGH SCHOOL (WHITTIER)

Far from Hollywood, California, Whittier High School gained worldwide attention in 1985 when it was used as a location for the motion picture *Back to the Future*, starring Michael J. Fox. The campus was filmed again in 1989 for Fox's *Back to the Future II*.

The Whittier High School campus, 12417 Philadelphia Street, Whittier, California. (Photograph taken in 1989.)

This school is also a part of U.S. history, having been attended by Richard M. Nixon, the 37th president of the United States.

Whittier High School is located at 12417 Philadelphia Street, north of Whittier Boulevard and east of the San Gabriel Valley Freeway (605) in Whittier, California. Map Code: 677 C6.

Shipyards

Todd Pacific Shipyards Corporation (Los Angeles)

TODD PACIFIC SHIPYARDS CORPORATION (LOS ANGELES)

The Todd Pacific Shipyards Corporation, Los Angeles Division, in San Pedro, California, was not a frequent location for motion pictures when it was operational. Now closed, the future of the massive facility is unknown.

The shipyard is included in this book as it was a location for one 1993 motion picture and a background location in another.

Opposite Top: The Todd Pacific Shipyards in the San Pedro District of Los Angeles, a location in *Men Don't Tell* (1993). (Photograph taken in 1986.)

Opposite Bottom: A view of the Todd Pacific Shipyards from Vineland Place, the location of several scenes from *Men Don't Tell* (1993) and *Colors* (1988). (Photograph taken in 1986.)

« Colors »

Actor Dennis Hopper turns director in this 1988 action-drama starring Sean Penn and Robert Duvall as Los Angeles cops who work a gang detail and confront the city's worst juveniles and young adults.

This shipyard is a background location and can be seen in the distance as a search warrant is served for a murder suspect in a house on a San Pedro hill.

« Men Don't Tell »

This 1993 motion picture addresses spousal abuse from the perspective of a physically and emotionally battered husband (Peter Strauss).

This shipyard is the location where Strauss owns a ship repair business. It is also in another scene, in the background of the house of one of Strauss' relatives living in the San Pedro hills above this facility.

The Todd Pacific Shipyards Corp., Los Angeles Division, is located at 710 N. Front Street.

The houses are located on Vineland Place.

Both locations are north of the Harbor Freeway (110), in the San Pedro District of Los Angeles, California. Map Code: 824 C3.

Stairways

3rd Street Tunnel Stairway (Los Angeles)

Much of the city of Los Angeles is hilly, as are many of the cities and towns that make up the greater Los Angeles area. Streets and roadways, narrow and wide, twist and turn through the hills, valleys and canyons of the majority of residential neighborhoods.

To have pedestrian access from one street to another in many neighborhoods, it became necessary to construct cement stairways, some consisting of but a few steps, but many much longer and very steep.

The majority of these stairways were built in the 1920s and 1930s. Some remain, still serving the community. Many, however, have disappeared, the victims of time and progress.

3RD STREET TUNNEL STAIRWAY (LOS ANGELES)

A stairway near the 3rd Street Tunnel is a location in many segments of the following motion pictures.

Looking west from 3rd Street, across Hill Street to the 3rd Street Tunnel in downtown Los Angeles. The site of the long cement stairway seen in many films is immediately right of the tunnel's entrance. (Photograph taken in 1998.)

« Night Has a Thousand Eyes »

The plot of this 1948 film was previously addressed in the Railroad Stations chapter of this book.

The long cement stairway, located on the north side of the Hill Street entrance to the 3rd Street tunnel, ascended to Clay Alley, then to the top of Bunker Hill, where it ended. Several multistory wood houses, dating to the early part of the century, were converted to rooming houses in the 1930s and 1940s.

In this motion picture, Edward G. Robinson walks up and down the stairway many times to his room located in one of the rooming houses.

The cement stairway, the houses and Clay Alley (previously mentioned in the Alleys chapter) were all demolished in the 1960s, 1970s and 1980s because of extensive construction on Bunker Hill.

« *The Glenn Miller Story* »

The plot of this 1954 film was previously addressed in the Alleys chapter.

The stairway is a location in the opening scenes as Glenn Miller (James Stewart) walks up it to Clay Alley and the East Los Angeles Loan Company to claim his trombone.

« *The Indestructible Man* »

The plot of this 1956 motion picture was previously addressed in the Buildings chapter.

The stairway is the location in one scene in the film wherein a man who "Butcher" Benton (Lon Chaney, Jr.) is stalking walks up it to the top and to death at the hands of Benton.

The site of this stairway is north (to the right) of the Hill Street entrance to the 3rd Street Tunnel, now covered by an apartment complex. Map Code: 634 F4.

Streets

Canon Drive (Beverly Hills)
Hollywood Boulevard (Hollywood)
Olvera Street (Los Angeles)
Santa Fe Avenue (Los Angeles)

The streets of the city of Los Angeles, especially in Hollywood, have served as locations for motion pictures since the early 1920s. Many streets of that era have been widened and some have disappeared from the landscape due to developments and improvements in various communities. Some, however, remain virtually unchanged from the time of filming.

Segments of the following motion pictures and television series were filmed on streets throughout the greater Los Angeles area.

CANON DRIVE (BEVERLY HILLS)

Canon Drive, lined with majestic date and Washingtonia palm trees in Beverly Hills, curves through that affluent community and is a favorite location of film production companies.

Canon Drive, between Carmelita Avenue and Santa Monica Boulevard in Beverly Hills. (Photograph taken in 1984.)

« A Chump at Oxford »

Laurel and Hardy again drive down Canon Drive, approximately in the same location as in *Busy Bodies* (1936) in this 1940 motion picture, their 94th together and their 61st talkie. This time, however, they are in a limousine driven by a chauffeur (James Millican) who gives them a lift to the "Sterling Employment Agency."

« Columbo Cries Wolf »

Lieutenant Columbo (Peter Falk) investigates yet another murder in this 1990 television movie, this time in Beverly Hills and down Canon Drive.

« Pacific Heights »

Set in San Francisco, California, with some scenes in Beverly Hills, this 1990 thriller stars Melanie Griffith and Matthew Modine as a young couple who buy a Victorian house, fix it up, then rent out two of its apartments—one to a sociopath (Michael Keaton).

Griffith's mother (Tippi Hedren) plays a Beverly Hills socialite.

Several scenes were filmed on Canon Drive.

« Menendez: A Killing in Beverly Hills »

The events leading to the grisly murders of the parents of Erik and Lyle Menendez, crimes both Erik and Lyle were convicted of, are the focus of this 1994 television movie.

Canon Drive is the location in one scene wherein Erik drives an expensive sports car down it toward a meeting with a friend.

This Canon Drive motion picture location is north of Santa Monica Boulevard and east of the San Diego Freeway (405). Map Code: 632 F1.

HOLLYWOOD BOULEVARD (HOLLYWOOD)

Hollywood Boulevard, without question, is one of the most famous streets in the world, made so by regular references in motion pictures, television series, magazines and newspapers by newspaper and television columnists. In addition, the intersection of Hollywood and Vine remains popular today, decades after it was made world-famous by visiting servicemen and servicewomen during World War II.

Segments of the following motion pictures were filmed on this street.

« Hollywood Boulevard »

John Halliday stars as a bitter former movie star who writes his memoirs for a sleaze magazine and creates embarrassment for his daughter (Marsha Hunt) and a former lover (Esther Ralston).

The boulevard is seen regularly throughout this 1936 release.

The 6600 block of world-famous Hollywood Boulevard. (Photograph taken in 1990.)

« Crazy House »

Comedians Ole Olsen and Chick Johnson take over a movie studio (Universal Studios) to make a musical comedy in this 1943 motion picture. Many guest stars appear, including Basil Rathbone and Nigel Bruce in a cameo as Sherlock Holmes and Dr. Watson.

The boulevard is the location of a big parade heralding the arrival of Olsen and Johnson in Hollywood to do the film.

« Another You »

A compulsive liar (Gene Wilder) is finally released from a sanitarium in the care of street hustler Richard Pryor as part of Pryor's court-ordered community service program. Together, the two immediately get involved in a scam.

238 STREETS

Several scenes of this 1991 motion picture were shot on this boulevard.

« Born into Exile »

In this 1997 television movie, two teens (Mark-Paul Gosselaar and Gina Philips), in conflict with their parents, run away from their rural homes and go to Los Angeles, where they are forced to live on the street.

This street, near the Supply Sergeant Building, is the location where both begged money in the rain from strangers.

As a note of interest, the world-famous Brown Derby restaurant is located on the northwest corner of the intersection of Hollywood and Vine.

The intersection of Hollywood and Vine and the area of Hollywood Boulevard seen as locations in these films are west of the Hollywood Freeway (101) in Hollywood, California. Map Code: 593 E4 and F4.

OLVERA STREET (LOS ANGELES)

Olvera Street is one of the oldest streets in Los Angeles. Formerly known as Vine Street and Wine Street, it officially became Olvera Street in 1877 by a city ordinance to honor Agustin Olvera, the first judge of the county of Los Angeles.

Increasingly neglected over the decades, it became a dirty alley with dilapidated buildings until 1926 when it was paved and refurbished by concerned citizens.

The street was closed to through vehicular traffic by another city ordinance in 1929 and opened as a Mexican marketplace on April 20, 1930.

As with the Los Angeles Police Department's academy, this street has one of the barrack buildings that housed athletes in the Olympic Village during the 1932 Olympic games held in Los Angeles. It is located at E-6 Olvera Street and is occupied by the Casa Suzanna.

Currently, over two million visitors each year come to this location.

The street, even though generally crowded, is a favorite location for motion picture and television series production companies.

The north entrance to Olvera Street, looking south from Macy Street toward Plaza Park. (Photograph taken in 1998.)

Segments of the following productions were filmed at this location.

« *Lethal Weapon 3* »

The plot of this 1992 motion picture was previously addressed in the Parks chapter of this book.
This street is the scene of an armored car robbery.

« *Dragnet* »
(1951–1959/1967–1970)

The plot of this television series was previously addressed in the City Halls chapter.

The south entrance to Olvera Street, looking north from Plaza Park toward Macy Street, is the location of the historic wooden cross (replica) installed to commemorate the city's 148th birthday in 1929. (Photograph taken in 1998.)

The opening scene of the 1968 Christmas episode was filmed at this location.

Olvera Street is located south of Macy Street, between Main and Alameda streets, north of the historic Pueblo De Los Angeles Plaza (The Plaza) which is east of the Harbor Freeway (110) and north of the Hollywood Freeway (101) in downtown Los Angeles. Map Code: 634 G3.

SANTA FE AVENUE (LOS ANGELES)

Santa Fe Avenue, between the 1st Street Viaduct and the 7th Street Viaduct near downtown Los Angeles, parallels the Santa Fe Railroad tracks and is a primary thoroughfare for hundreds of trucks each day

Santa Fe Avenue near downtown Los Angeles, looking north toward the 4th Street Viaduct. (Photograph taken in 1998.)

carrying cargo to and from the many warehouses located on each side of the avenue. The avenue is also a favorite location for motion picture and television series chase scene segments, especially those involving police cars and the cars of the bad guys.

The plots of all of the following motion pictures were previously addressed in the Bridges chapter, and various scenes from the motion pictures were filmed on this avenue. All locations are in Map Code: 634 H4, H5 and H6.

« *The Naked Gun: From the Files of Police Squad* »

This 1988 screwball comedy has a chase scene on Santa Fe Avenue near the 4th Street Viaduct.

Looking west from Santa Fe Avenue, near the 1st Street Viaduct and the 1st Street location of the shoot-out scene in *Stop! or My Mom Will Shoot* (1992). (Photograph taken in 1998.)

« Police Academy 6: City Under Siege »

Near the conclusion of this 1989 comedy, a police pursuit comes down this avenue and goes under the 4th Street Viaduct.

« Predator 2 »

As this 1990 film concludes, a space ship carrying a group of predators takes off for outer space, leaving a long, wide gouge in the earth and a dazed Danny Glover waiting for help that quickly arrives, traveling south on this avenue from the 1st Street Viaduct.

The location of this activity is east of Santa Fe Avenue, between the 1st Street and the 4th Street viaducts.

« *Wedlock* »

The plot of this 1991 motion picture was previously addressed in the Rivers chapter.

Rutger Hauer, fleeing the police, speeds down Santa Fe Avenue, then turns into the "*Them!* Tunnel" and escapes through a storm drain, eventually surfacing in the middle of this street near the 6th Street Viaduct.

« *Stop! or My Mom Will Shoot* »

Two scenes from this 1992 release were filmed on the avenue.

The first is where Estelle Getty buys a gun; the second, where Getty and her son (Sylvester Stallone) get into a shoot-out with bad guys.

« *Fast Company* »

This avenue is the location of a horrific vehicle explosion under the 4th Street Viaduct in this 1995 movie.

« *In the Line of Duty: Kidnapped* »

This 1995 motion picture has one scene filmed on this avenue.

« *A Face to Die For* »

This 1996 motion picture opens and closes on Santa Fe Avenue under the 4th Street Viaduct.

Subways

Los Angeles MTA Subway System (Los Angeles)

Los Angeles MTA Subway System (Los Angeles)

The city of Los Angeles finally began construction on a subway system in the 1980s, much to the delight of the citizens weary of freeway congestion but quite to the dismay of those fearful of disaster that could be caused by an earthquake. The system, however, did survive the major quake in 1994 with minimal damage, and construction continues.

Soon after the system expanded from the initial station beneath the massive Union Station complex to the heart of the city at Pershing Square, a small park nestled between rows of skyscrapers, film crews from production companies began to utilize this new transportation system to film a variety of segments for upcoming productions.

« Predator 2 »

The plot of this 1990 motion picture was previously addressed in the Buildings and Streets chapters of this book.

The subway station and the tunnel east of the station beneath Union

The Los Angeles MTA subway system's Union Station Terminal, beneath the massive Union Station railroad terminal in downtown Los Angeles. (Photograph taken in 1998.)

Station is the location where gang members harassed passengers and where the creature suddenly appeared and attacked everyone in sight.

« *Speed* »

The plot of this 1994 motion picture was previously addressed in the City Halls chapter.

This subway system is used extensively in the last part of this film as Keanu Reeves struggles with Dennis Hopper to keep Hopper from triggering a device that will destroy a section of the subway system.

The area of the subway used to film this lengthy scene is between the station located under the city's Union Station and the Pershing Square station.

Reeves and Hopper have a desperate fight on top of the subway train as it races out-of-control, resulting in Hopper's death.

« *Brave New World* »

The novel by Aldous Huxley comes to the screen in this 1998 motion picture that features a futuristic world and its leaders, one being Leonard Nimoy.

The subway is featured as trains deliver workers to a large factory.

The subway system begins at the Union Station and extends under the city in a southwest direction to Pershing Square, then west toward MacArthur Park. Map Code: 634 G3 & F4.

Theaters

Mann's Chinese Theater (Hollywood)
Wiltern Theater (Los Angeles)

Once ranking a close second to New York City in number of theaters, the Los Angeles area, profuse with these centers of entertainment, lost hundreds of the buildings when the television industry boomed shortly after the conclusion of World War II.

Still, many remain, and a few have been locations for motion picture segments.

MANN'S CHINESE THEATER (HOLLYWOOD)

One, Mann's (formerly Grauman's) Chinese Theater, is a major tourist attraction.

The following motion picture theaters are locations for segments of the listed motion pictures.

Mann's (Grauman's) Chinese Theater was opened by showman Sid Grauman on May 18, 1927. The feature motion picture shown that day was Cecil B. DeMille's *King of Kings* (1927).

The architecture is colorful Chinese, but this building is known worldwide for its forecourt, where the hand and footprints of famous movie stars

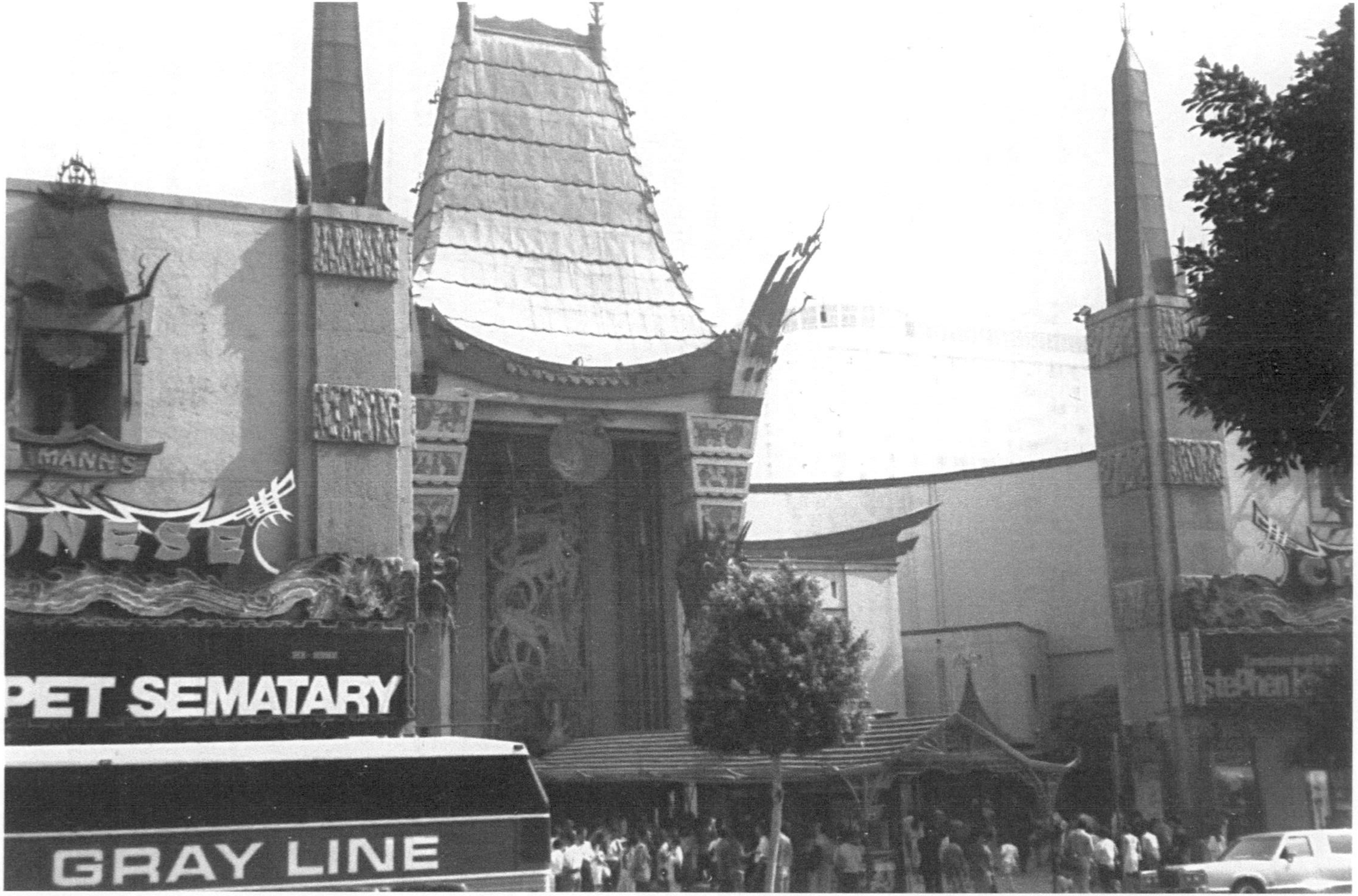
MANN'S
NESE
PET SEMATARY
GRAY LINE

are preserved in cement. The complex is #55 in the city's Historic-Cultural Monuments listing.

« What Price Hollywood? »

Based on a story by author Adela Rogers St. Johns, this 1932 drama, an inspiration for the later *A Star Is Born* motion pictures (1937, 1954 and 1976), features Lowell Sherman as a director fighting alcoholism who meets a Brown Derby waitress (Constance Bennett) and makes her a star.

This theater is in one lengthy segment near the beginning of the film wherein Sherman brings Bennett to a gala premier in an old car shortly after meeting her at the famous restaurant.

« Star Dust »

The plot of this 1940 motion picture was previously addressed in the Railroad Stations chapter.

The theater is the location of a movie premier in the film.

« Variety Girl »

The plot of this 1947 film was previously addressed in the Movie Studios chapter.

The theater is one of many sites visited by Mary Hatcher and Olga San Juan after their arrival in Hollywood.

« Singin' in the Rain »

Considered by many film critics as the greatest Hollywood musical of all time, this 1952 release features Gene Kelly and Donald O'Connor as established film stars adjusting to the arrival of talking motion pictures in 1927 Hollywood. Debbie Reynolds costars as a struggling actress hoping to break into films.

Opposite: **Mann's (Grauman's) Chinese Theater, 6925 Hollywood Boulevard, Hollywood, is a tourist attraction and a popular film location. (Photograph taken in 1989.)**

The theater is a location on two segments of the film, the first as the film opens at the premier of *The Royal Rascal*, which is attended by many stars, including Gene Kelly and Donald O'Connor.

The second appearance comes near the end of the film when yet another premier is held, this time *The Dancing Cavalier* starring Gene Kelly.

« *Won Ton Ton, the Dog Who Saved Hollywood* »

The plot of this 1976 motion picture was previously addressed in the Movie Studios chapter of this book.

The theater is a location in the opening scene of this film wherein Won Ton Ton's pawprints are put in cement in the forecourt.

« *Twins* »

In this 1988 comedy, Arnold Schwarzenegger and Danny DeVito star as genetically designed twin brothers who find each other 35 years after birth.

The theater is one location visited by the two as they get to know each other.

« *Forrest Gump* »

Tom Hanks stars as a slow-witted man who ploughs through life, from the rise of Elvis Presley to the fall of President Richard M. Nixon, and even survives the horrors of the Vietnam conflict as a soldier.

This theater is one location seen by Hanks on a Hollywood visit in this 1994 film.

« *Speed* »

The plot of this 1994 action film was previously addressed in the City Halls chapter.

Keanu Reeves and Sandra Bullock are trapped on a runaway subway train racing through tunnels under Los Angeles. Their lives are spared as the train crashes into a construction zone under Hollywood Boulevard and catapults to the surface through the unfinished section of the Hollywood station, skidding to a stop in front of this theater, much to the delight of Reeves and Bullock and a large group of tourists.

« A Dangerous Affair »

The theater is a primary location in the plot of this 1995 movie starring Connie Sellecca as a government executive desperately seeking protection from a stalker (Gregory Harrison) with whom she had a romance.

« The Price of Love »

Peter Facinelli stars as a teen, disowned by his parents, who comes to Los Angeles for a better life but soon turns to prostitution to survive in this 1995 film.

The theater is a location where a group of teens hang out on the sidewalk and beg money from passing pedestrians.

« I Love Lucy » (1951–1957)

This extremely popular television series was previously discussed in the Houses chapter.

The theater is a location in episode #128, "Lucy Visits Grauman's," which was telecast nationally on October 3, 1955.

Note: All forecourt scenes in this episode were filmed at the Desilu Studios.

Mann's Chinese Theater is located at 6925 Hollywood Boulevard in Hollywood, west of the Hollywood Freeway (101). Map Code: 593 D4.

WILTERN THEATER (LOS ANGELES)

The Wiltern Theater is a typical 1930s-style movie theater that still serves the residents of the Wilshire District of Los Angeles. Scheduled for demolition in 1980, it was saved, refurbished to retain its art deco atmosphere and reopened.

A favorite location for motion picture production companies, it became and remains famous as the site of an important segment of the 1987 motion picture *La Bamba*, which was based on the life of rock 'n' roll idol Ritchie Valens.

Segments of the following motion picture were filmed inside and outside of this theater.

« *The Jacksons: An American Dream* »

Twenty actors portray Michael Jackson and his brothers in this 1992 television movie that follows the singing group from their start in Gary, Indiana, to their famous "Victory" tour in 1984.

This theater is one of many the group performed at in this film.

The Wiltern Theater is located at 3970 Wilshire Boulevard in Los Angeles, California, north of the Santa Monica Freeway (10). Map Code: 633 H2.

Opposite: The marquee and facade of the Wiltern Theater. (Photograph taken in 1989.)

Town Squares

Sierra Madre Town Square (Sierra Madre)

    The traditional town square, so common in towns and villages in the 18th, the 19th and the early part of the 20th century, is fading from the American landscape.

    It is rare to find a town square away from a motion picture studio back lot that is a location in a motion picture segment. One such town square was found and identified as an integral location in a classic sci-fi flick and a later drama.

SIERRA MADRE TOWN SQUARE (SIERRA MADRE)

« Race Against Time: The Search for Sarah »

    The plot of this 1996 motion picture was previously addressed in the Bridges chapter of this book.

    The Sierra Madre Town Square is the location of the carjacking and kidnapping of the daughter of Patty Duke and Richard Crenna.

TOWN SQUARES   255

The Sierra Madre, California, town square at Baldwin Avenue and Sierra Madre Boulevard. (Photograph taken in 1988.)

The Sierra Madre town square is located at the intersection of Sierra Madre Boulevard and Baldwin Avenue in Sierra Madre, California, north of the Foothill Freeway (210). Map Code: 567 A2.

Training Centers

Naval Training Center (San Diego)

Eighty miles south of Los Angeles is San Diego, a city famous for many things, including a mild climate, but especially for the training centers for future marines and naval personnel.

NAVAL TRAINING CENTER (SAN DIEGO)

One of the two training facilities, the Naval Training Center (NTC) and its Recruit Training Command (RTC), was phased out, and the base officially closed in 1997.

Opened in 1923, this huge 500-acre complex trained recruits and other naval personnel for a future in this branch of military service.

As Hollywood was nearby, production companies often took advantage of this center for location filming for films with a U.S. Navy theme, especially during the days of World War II.

Segments of the following motion pictures were filmed at this facility.

TRAINING CENTERS 257

The Lytton Avenue (Gate 1) entrance to the training center, a location in many films. (Photograph taken in 1997.)

« *Here Comes the Navy* »

The battleship U.S.S. *Arizona*, destined to become a national shrine when sunk on December 7, 1941, is the centerpiece of this 1934 motion picture starring James Cagney and Pat O'Brien as sailors who hate each other, especially when Cagney dates O'Brien's sister (Gloria Stuart).

Cagney and other recruits enter this facility through Gate 1, then stop at the flagpole just inside the gate to watch a flag-raising ceremony.

Later, Cagney and fellow recruits do a series of gun drills to music on Preble Parade Field, then march across the field during graduation ceremonies.

The training center's Preble Parade Field, where the Andrews Sisters performed in the 1941 film *In the Navy* and the location of James Cagney's training and graduation in the 1934 film *Here Comes the Navy*. (Photograph taken in 1997.)

« *In the Navy* »

A typical Abbott and Costello pre–World War II comedy, this 1941 motion picture finds the two comedians in basic training at this center before being assigned to a ship and nearly destroying the Navy. Dick Powell and the Andrews Sisters costar.

The plaque at the Lytton Avenue (Gate 1) entrance to the center is in one scene as are the large guns situated along Cushing Road, a location where Patty Andrews kissed Dick Powell. The adjoining Preble Parade Field is the location where the Andrews Sisters performed to a large assembly of sailors. The old flagpole just inside Gate 1 is also a location seen in this film.

The deck guns near Preble Parade Field, the location where Patty Andrews kissed Dick Powell in the 1941 film, *In the Navy*. (Photograph taken in 1997.)

« The Fleet's In »

A wartime musical, this 1942 motion picture stars William Holden as a sailor pursuing lovely Dorothy Lamour. This film was also the debut of "The Blonde Bombshell," Betty Hutton, who became an instant star.

This film was later remade as *Sailor Beware* in 1951.

The Gate 1 entrance of the center is a location in this film as is the Preble Parade Field.

« Star Spangled Rhythm »

The plot of this 1942 motion picture was previously addressed in the Movie Studios chapter of this book.

The Preble Parade Field and Gate 1 are also locations in this film.

The cement base of the training center's original flagpole, a location in many films, including the 1934 release *Here Comes the Navy*. (Photograph taken in 1997.)

« *Follow the Boys* »

An all-star cast headed by George Raft travel "everywhere" to entertain servicemen and servicewomen in this 1944 wartime motion picture.

Several locations in the training center are seen in the film, including the Gate 1 entrance, the Preble Parade Field and the boxing arena (next to the Preble Parade Field, later the site of a bowling center). This boxing arena is the "stage" where Sophie Tucker and the Andrews Sisters perform musical numbers.

The famous plaque located at the Lytton Avenue (Gate 1) entrance to the San Diego Naval Training Center. (Photograph taken in 1997.)

« Sailor Beware »

This 1951 remake of *The Fleet's In* (1942) stars Dean Martin and Jerry Lewis as sailors and follows the two comedians from their training days to an assignment on a ship at sea.

The center's Gate 1 and the Preble Parade Field are primary locations in this motion picture.

Note: As this massive naval facility is soon to be redeveloped into a recreational and housing area, permission to enter must be asked at Gate 1 (Lytton Avenue, south of Rosecrans Street) or at Gate 3 (Roosevelt Road and Rosecrans Street).

The Naval Training Center is located in San Diego, California. Map Code: 1268 E6 (Gate 1), D7 (Gate 3) in the San Diego Edition.

Tunnels

2nd Street Tunnel (Los Angeles)
3rd Street Tunnel (Los Angeles)
Them! *Tunnel (Los Angeles)*

The city of Los Angeles has many tunnels, most for vehicular traffic, a few for pedestrians and some for access to areas of city and county property for repair or improvement purposes. More tunnels are being dug and more are planned as the city's subway system expands.

The following tunnels have proved to be favorite locations for motion picture and television series production companies.

All scenes are of vehicles traveling through the tunnels, except where noted.

2ND STREET TUNNEL (LOS ANGELES)

The 2nd Street Tunnel in downtown Los Angeles is the most popular tunnel in the metropolitan area for motion picture and television series segments and for segments of hundreds of commercials.

« The Night That Panicked America »

Solely based on the re-creation of the events leading up to the famous radio broadcast of October 30, 1938, this 1975 motion picture stars Paul Shenar as Orson Welles, the producer and lead actor in the broadcast based on H.G. Wells novel *The War of the Worlds*, about a Martian invasion of earth.

Presented in a news bulletin format, this radio broadcast actually did panic many persons across the United States.

In the film, the tunnel is where a despondent man gets out of his car and sits on the curb, expecting his life to end by the ray guns of the Martian invaders.

« Young Doctors in Love »

This 1982 movie is rife with hospital comedy, revolving around the day-to-day mishaps encountered by the staff of a big city medical facility.

Many soap opera stars appear in cameo roles. Demi Moore, Michael McKean and Sean Young star.

« One Dark Night »

A shocking tale of horror, this 1983 release finds a sorority pledge (Meg Tilly) facing a final hurdle to gaining acceptance—to spend the night in a dark mausoleum.

« Heartbreakers »

Peter Coyote and Nick Mancuso star in this 1984 motion picture as an artist (Coyote) and a businessman (Mancuso) who try to define their relationship with each other.

Many Los Angeles locations in this film, including this tunnel.

« The Terminator »

This 1984 film features Arnold Schwarzenegger as a cyborg sent from the future to kill a woman (Linda Hamilton).

« The Annihilator »

In this 1986 thriller, a newspaperman (Mark Lindsay Chapman) is hunted by humanoid robots, including a clone of his girlfriend (Catherine Mary Stewart), programmed to kill him.

« Police Story: The Freeway Killings »

Los Angeles Police Department Deputy Chief Bob Devers (Richard Crenna) and Officer Anne Cavanaugh (Angie Dickinson) are hot on the trail of serial slayers in this 1987 motion picture with a subplot dealing with corrupt cops.

« Jack's Back »

London's "Jack the Ripper" has his style copied by a serial killer in present day Los Angeles in this 1988 thriller.
The tunnel is a location near the end of this film.

« The Case of the Hillside Stranglers »

The plot of this 1989 motion picture was previously addressed in the Courts chapter of this book.
This tunnel is the location where Buono (Dennis Farina) and Bianchi (Billy Zane), posing as police officers, stopped a woman (Karen Austin) for speeding and attempted to force her out of her car. Both left and her life was saved when she demanded more identification from the two men, who were not wearing police uniforms.

« Sneakers »

The tunnel is in San Francisco where a Russian diplomat is assassinated in this 1992 motion picture.
Robert Redford is the leader of a high-tech security organization attempting to locate a super decoder before the Russians get it out of the country.
Sidney Poitier costars.

« *The Disappearance of Christina* »

John Stamos, Robert Carradine and Kim Delaney star in this 1993 movie, the plot of which centers on a wealthy businessman arrested after his wife disappears during a voyage on the yacht of a friend.

« *Another Midnight Run* »

The plot of this 1994 release was previously addressed in the City Halls chapter of this book.
The tunnel is in two lengthy scenes in the film.

« *Ed McBain's 87th Precinct* »

Randy Quaid and Alex McArthur portray homicide detectives after a suspect wanted for the ritual murders of young female track stars.
This 1995 movie is based on McBain's novel *Lightning*.

« *Independence Day* »

The plot of this 1996 sci-fi adventure was previously addressed in the Bridges chapter.
The tunnel is the location in the film where people are running from a giant wall of flames.

« *Money Talks* »

The plot of this 1997 motion picture was previously addressed in the Bridges chapter of this book.
The tunnel is a location in one lengthy scene.

« *On the Line* »

The plot of this 1998 motion picture was previously addressed in the Buildings chapter.

The Hill Street entrance to the 2nd Street Tunnel in downtown Los Angeles. (Photograph taken in 1998.)

The tunnel is a location in a lengthy scene near the end of this film where the gang of teenage bank robbers were pursued by the police, both in black-and-white cars, detective cars and a helicopter.

« *Downtown* » *(1986–1987)*

This television series features a Los Angeles cop (Michael Nouri) assigned to supervise a diverse group of parolees.

The tunnel is a location in a 1986 episode centering on a man who persuaded one of the parolees (Blair Underwood) to quit a street gang and is killed.

« Heart of the City » (1986)

The tunnel is a location in a 1986 episode of this television series that centers on problems at a local birth control clinic.

« Jake and the Fatman » (1986–1992)

The plot of this television series was previously addressed in the City Halls chapter of this book.

The tunnel is a location in a 1988 episode.

The 2nd Street Tunnel is beneath the Bunker Hill District of Los Angeles, in the downtown area, between Hill Street and Figueroa Street. Map Code: 634 F3.

3RD STREET TUNNEL (LOS ANGELES)

The 3rd Street Tunnel, one block south of the 2nd Street Tunnel, is not as popular a location for motion picture and television series segments as the 2nd Street Tunnel, but has been filmed many times over the years.

The area directly above this tunnel (also known as the Hill Street Tunnel) was a favorite film location for the Hal Roach Studios in the silent era of motion pictures.

Props were built on the hillside above the tunnel (then two tunnels—one for streetcars and one for vehicles) to allow the camera angle to give the illusion of height.

In Harold Lloyd's 1918 motion picture, *Look Out Below*, the famous actor and his girlfriend were on the steel beams of a building under construction, in reality just a few feet above the Hill Street entrance to this tunnel.

Two years later, Lloyd appeared as a drunk with a sleepwalking girl on the ledge of a tall apartment building in the 1920 motion picture, *High and Dizzy*, also filmed just a few feet above the Hill Street entrance to this tunnel.

268 TUNNELS

The Hill Street entrance to the 3rd Street Tunnel in downtown Los Angeles. (Photograph taken in 1998.)

Segments of the following motion pictures were filmed in this tunnel, primarily for vehicle segments unless otherwise noted.

« *Police Academy 2: Their First Assignment* »

This 1985 comedy is the sequel to *Police Academy* (1984) and follows the screwball bunch of cops, led by Steve Guttenberg and Bubba Smith, on their first assignment in the field.
The Flower Street entrance to this tunnel is a location in this film.

« *Darkman* »

This 1990 release relates the story of a disfigured scientist (Liam Neeson) who recovers from the injuries that nearly cost him his life and who then disguises himself in synthetic skin and goes after those responsible.

The west end (Flower Street) of the tunnel can also be seen in this film.

The 3rd Street Tunnel is beneath the Bunker Hill District of Los Angeles, in the downtown area, between Hill Street and Flower Street. Map Code: 634 F3 and 4.

THEM! TUNNEL (LOS ANGELES)

The only way this tunnel can be identified is to label it the *Them!* Tunnel as it was made famous in lengthy scenes from the 1954 sci-fi thriller *Them!*

The tunnel has no name simply because it is a low and narrow access tunnel from Santa Fe Avenue to the nearby Los Angeles River, under the 6th Street Viaduct.

Segments of the following motion pictures and television series productions were filmed at this tunnel.

« *The Naked Gun: From the Files of Police Squad* »

The plot of this 1988 comedy was previously addressed in the Bridges chapter of this book.

The tunnel is a location in one lengthy pursuit scene in the film.

« *L.A. Story* »

Steven Martin portrays a meteorologist living and working in Los Angeles, going from one romantic involvement to another in this 1991 romantic comedy.

« *Wedlock* »

The plot of this 1991 movie was previously addressed in the Rivers chapter of this book.

Beneath the 6th Street Viaduct, looking east down the ramp leading to the entrance to the *Them!* Tunnel and the Los Angeles River. (Photograph taken in 1998.)

Rutger Hauer, fleeing the police, turns his car into this tunnel and eventually escapes through a storm drain.

« *Doppelganger: The Evil Within* »

Drew Barrymore stars in a dual role as a "good" girl on the run from her evil ghostly double in this 1993 thriller. George Newbern costars as a Los Angeles writer who becomes deeply involved with Barrymore.

Near the end of the film, Newbern is chased into this tunnel by a man with a knife.

« Beverly Hills Cop III »

The plot of this 1994 sequel was previously addressed in the City Halls chapter.
The tunnel is the location of a pursuit scene.

« CHiPs »
(1977–1983)

This television action series featured the on-duty and off-duty adventures of fictional motorcycle-riding officers of the California Highway Patrol (CHiPs for short).
The tunnel is the location in many chase and car race scenes in several episodes.

« Unsolved Mysteries »
(1988–1997)

The plot of this television series was previously addressed in the Churches chapter of this book.
The Santa Fe Avenue entrance to this tunnel, under the 6th Street Viaduct, is a Cleveland, Ohio, location of a "Black Dahlia"–type murder investigated by Eliot Ness in the 1930s in a 1993 episode of this series.
The *Them!* Tunnel is located east of Santa Fe Avenue, leading into the Los Angeles River beneath the 6th Street Viaduct, in downtown Los Angeles, north of the Santa Monica Freeway (10). Map Code: 634 H5.

Index

Numbers in **boldface** refer to pages with photographs.

A & M Records 127
Aaker, Lee 196
Abbott, Bud 32, 33, 137, 141, 143, 200, 258
The Abbott and Costello Show (TV) 137
The Abyss (1989) 25
Academy Awards 18, 19
Ace Comics 113
The Adventures of Brisco County, Jr. (TV) 54, **142**
The Adventures of Marco Polo (1938) 199
Airwolf (TV) 108
The Alamo 44, 154
Alcott, Louisa May 121
Allyson, June 195
Alpert, Herb 127
Alyn, Kirk 54
The Amazing Colossal Man (1957) 144
Amazing Stories (TV) 43, 44, 154
Ambassador Hotel 98, 99
Ameche, Don 9
Amelia Earhart: The Final Flight (1994) 35
The American President (1995) 113
Anaconda (1997) 114
Anchors Aweigh (1945) 15, **16**, 129
Anderson, Eddie "Rochester" 190
Anderson, Loni 73
Anderson, Pamela 97
Andrews, Dana 70, 201
Andrews, Patty 258, 259

Andrews Sisters 258, 260
Angel's Flight 13, 35, 177, **178**, **179**, 180, 181
Anjac Building 34, 38, **39**, 41
Annie Oakley (TV) 202
The Annihilator (1986) 212, 264
Another 48 HRS. (1990) 72
Another Midnight Run (1990) 72, 265
Another You (1991) 237
Arboretum of Los Angeles County 109, 112, 113, 114, 149, 150, 181, **182**
Arch Rock 197, **203**
Arden Villa 117, **119**
U.S.S. *Arizona* 257
Arkin, Adam 78
Arnaz, Desi 132
Astaire, Fred 130
"At the Ball, That's All" (song) 205
Atherton, William 134
Atwill, Lionel 51
Auston, Karen 264
Autry, Gene 204, 206
Avalon Boys Quartet 205

The Bachelor and the Bobby-Soxer (1947) 219, **221**
Back to the Future (1985) 226
Back to the Future II (1989) 226
Bacon, Kevin 37
Baer, Parley 132
Baio, Scott 223
Baird, Jeanne 71

Baker, Carroll 184
Bakula, Scott 26
Baldwin, Daniel 75
Ball, Lucille 104, 131
Barbera, Joseph 156
Barcroft, Roy 147
Barker, Lex 114
The Baron of Arizona (1950) 195
Barrie, James 128
Barrymore, Drew 270
Barton Fink (1991) 72
Basehart, Richard 70
Basinger, Kim 73, 77
Bateman, Jason 87
Bates Mansion 141, **142**
Bates Motel 141
Batman and Robin (1977) 107
Batman Forever (1995) 107
Batman's Bat Cave 54, 56
Bauer, Steven 97
Baxter, Meredith 121
Baywatch (TV) 108
Beatty, Warren 72
Beery, Noah 204
Beery, Wallace 11
Belushi, Jim 80
Ben-Hur (1926) 198
Bening, Annette 113
Bennett, Constance 249
Benny, Jack 190
Benzali, Daniel 83
Berkeley, Busby 95
Bernsen, Corbin 145
Best Seller (1987) 71
Bettger, Lyle 53
Beverly Hills City Hall 66, **68**, 69
Beverly Hills Cop III (1994) 67, 166, 271
Beverly Hills High School 218, **220, 221**
Beverly Hills High School Gymnasium 219, **221**
Beverly Hills 90210 (TV) 77, 108, 218
Bianchi, Kenneth 82, 94, 264
The Big Sombrero (1949) 206
Bierko, Craig 67
Biltmore Hotel 100, **101**, 102, 103
The Bionic Woman (TV) 108
Bissett, Jacqueline 118, 170
B.J. and the Bear (TV) 108
Black, Karen 134
Black Dahlia 80, 271
Blazing Saddles (1974) 155
Bleeth, Yasmine 29
Bleller, Andy 219
Blondie (TV) 137

Blondie Plays Cupid (1940) 187
Bloodlines: Murder in the Family (1993) 73
Blue of the Night (1932) 184
"Blue of the Night" (song) 185
Blue Thunder (TV) 108
The Bodyguard (1992) 73
Bogart, Humphrey 58, 199, 201
The Bold and the Beautiful (TV) 108
Born into Exile (1997) 238
Boyd, William 202
Boyer, Charles 94
Bracken, Eddie 133
Bradbury Building 34, 35, 36, **37**, 38
Bradshaw, Terry 103
Brave New World (1998) 246
Britton, Pamela 137
Broderick, Matthew 107
Bronson, Charles 118
Bronson Canyon 50, **52, 53, 54**, 56, 150
Brosnan, Pierce 162
Brown, Helen Gurley 69
Brown, Jim 196
Brown, Nicole 38, 176
Brown, Paul 69
Brown, Vanessa 114
Brown Derby Restaurant 238, 249
Bruce, Nigel 195, 237
Buck, Pearl 199
Bugsy (1991) 72, 128, 189
Bullock, Sandra 151, 163, 250, 251
Buono, Angelo 82, 88, 264
Burnette, Smiley 204, 206
A Burning Passion (1994) 36
Burr, Raymond 104
Busch, Mae 136
Busfield, Timothy 74
Busy Bodies (1933) 235
Buttafuoco, Joseph 165
Buttafuoco, Mary Jo 165

Cable Guy (1996) 107
Cagney, James 7, 185, 186, 199, 257, 258
Cagney & Lacey (TV) 79
California Arboretum Foundation 110
California Highway Patrol 271
Campbell, Bruce 54
Cannon (TV) 108, 147
Cannon, Dyan 108, 181
Canon Drive 234, **235**, 236
Cantor, Eddie 9
Career (1959) 133
Carillo, Leo 202
Carradine, David 110, 155

Carradine, Robert 265
Carrey, Jim 21, 31, 41, 77, 107
Carroll, Diahann 26
Carroll, John 203
Carter, Lynda 56
Casa Susanna 238
The Case of the Hillside Stranglers (1989) 82, 88, 94, 172, 264
Casnoff, Phillip 189
Casualities of Love: The Long Island Lollita Story (1993) 165
Central Park 150
Chamberlain, Richard 79
Chandler, Raymond 104
Chaney, Lon 69
Chaney, Lon, Jr. 35, 84, 137, 180, 233
Channing, Stockard 111
Chaplin (1992) 125
Chaplin, Charlie 125, 127, 198
Chapman, Mark Lindsay 264
Charlie Chaplin Studio (A&M Record Studio) 124, **125**, 127
Charlie's Angels (TV) 108
Chicago Hope (TV) 78
Chinatown (1974) 72
CHiPs (TV) 108, 271
Christmas in Connecticut (1992) 181, **182**
Christy, Dorothy 136
A Chump at Oxford (1940) 235
The Cisco Kid (TV) 202
Citizen Kane (1941) 128
Clarke, Mae 185, 186
Clay Alley 12, **13**, 14, 232, 233
Clift, Montgomery 107
Clinton, Bill (U.S. president) 219
Clooney, George 107
Coleman, Dabney 27, 111
Collins, Joan 119
Colorado (1940) 155
Colors (1988) 228, **229**, 230
Columbia Pictures Entertainment Studios 124, **126**, 127, 128
Columbo: Caution, Murder Can Be Hazardous to Your Health (1991) 173
Columbo Cries Wolf (1990) 235
Les Compères (1984) 77
Condor (1986) 213
Confessions: Two Faces of Evil (1994) 87, 89
Conrad, William 147
Conti, Tom 121
Conway, Pat 206
Cooper, Gary 183, 198, 199
Cops (1992) 118

Corrigan, Ray "Crash" 193, 203
Corrigan Ranch (Corriganville) 192, 193, 194, 195, **196**, 215, 217
Costello, Lou 32, 33, 137, 141, 143, 200, 258
Costner, Kevin 73
Coyote, Peter 263
Crabbe, Larry "Buster" 146, 147
Crampton, Barbara 161
Craven, James 147
Crazy Horse, Chief 201
Crazy House (1943) 237
Crenna, Richard 33, 82, 172, 254, 264
Criminal Behavior (1992) 145
Criminal Courts Building 81, 82, **83**, 84
Crockett, Davy 44
Crombie, Peter 145
Crosby, Bing 184, 185
Crowe, Russell 20
Crystal, Billy 76, 222, 223
Culver Studios **126**, 127
Cummings, Robert 200
Custer, George Armstrong 201

D'Abo, Olivia 223
Dallas (TV) 118, 132
Damone, Vic 26
A Dangerous Affair (1995) 251
Danielle Steele's "Star" (1993) 67
Danner, Blythe 105
Darkman (1990) 91, 268
Darling, Jean 123
Darnell, Linda 187
Dave (1993) 113
Davi, Robert 190
Davis, Bette 110, 172
Davis, Gail 202
The Day of the Locust (1975) 134
Dead-Bang (1989) 84
Dead Before Dawn (1993) 166
Dead Ringer (1964) 172
de Brulier, Nigel 203, 204
De Haven, Gloria 108
de Havilland, Olivia 94, 201
Delaney, Dana 80
Delaney, Kim 265
DeLuise, Peter 166
De Mille, Cecil B. 59, 247
de Neve, Felipe 153
Denier, Lydie 32
De Niro, Robert 72
Dennehy, Brian 71, 85, 102
Derek, Bo 22
Dern, Bruce 134

Desilu Studios 127, 251
Devane, William 85
Devil in a Blue Dress (1992) 145
DeVito, Danny 77, 222, 223, 250
Dickinson, Angie 264
Die Hard (1988) 72
Die Hard 2 (1990) 72
Dillon, Kevin 225
Dinah (the mule) 207
The Disappearance of Christina (1993) 265
Disney, Walt 58
Disney Studios (Walt Disney Studios) 223
The Distinguished Gentleman (1992) 84
Ditch and Live (1943) 49
Divine Madness (1980) 22
Dodger Studium 172
Dodsworth (1936) 103
Doherty, Shannen 36, 77, 157
Domergue, Faith 195
Donohoe, Amanda 74
Donor Unknown (1995) 36
Doppelganger: The Evil Within (1993) 270
Dorff, Stephen 166
Douglas, Kirk 36
Douglas, Melvyn 29
Douglas, Michael 113
Down Argentine Way (1940) 9
Downtown (TV) 266
Dracula (1931) 51, 141
Dragnet (TV) 69, 76, 172, 239
Drago, Billy 55
Drake, Tom 11
Draper, Polly 98
Dryer, Fred 78, 174
Duck Soup (1933) 118
Dude Cowboy (1941) 51
Dudikoff, Michael 166
Duke, Patty 33, 74, 254
Dumas, Alexandre 195
Dumbrille, Douglass 7
Duvall, Robert 106, 230
Dynasty (TV) 102, 118
Dynasty: The Reunion (1991) 102, 122

Earp, Wyatt 207
Eastham, Richard 206
Ed McBain's 87th Precinct (1995) 265
Eddy, Nelson 58, 59, 61, 62
Elam, Jack 114
Elephant Walk (1954) 201
The Elizabeth Taylor Story (1995) 107, 131, 135

Elizondo, Hector 32
Elroy, James 77
Emergency (TV) 55
Engle, Samuel G. 139
Eraser (1996) 75
Evans, Dale 202
Evans, Linda 119
Evanson, Kim 161
Evening Shade (TV) 103
Eye for an Eye (1996) **42**, 75

A Face in the Crowd (1957) 201
A Face to Die For (1996) 29, 243
Facinelli, Peter 251
Fahey, Jeff 37
Falk, Peter 173, 235
Fantasy Island Lagoon 109, **112**, 113
Farewell, My Lovely (1975) 104
Farina, Dennis 82, 88, 264
Fast and Loose (1939) 29
Fast Company (1995) 29, 91, 243
The Fat Man (1951) 101
Father's Day (1997) 76
Fawcett, Farrah 145
Federal Building 91
Fenn, Sherilyn 107
The Ferguson Affair (novel) 145
Ferris Bueller (TV) 108
Fibber McGee and Molly (radio) 9
Field, Sally 42, 75
Field, W.C. 33, 104
Field of Dreams (1989) 3
Final Analysis (1992) 73
Finlayson, James 205
1st Street Viaduct 23, 24, 26, 185, 186, 187, 213, 240, **242**
Fisher, Amy 165
Fisher, Eddie 107
Flamingo Casino 72
Flash Gordon (serial) (1936) 146
Flash Gordon Conquers the Universe (serial) (1940) 147
Flash Gordon's Trip to Mars (serial) (1938) 146
The Fleet's In (1942) 259, 261
Fletcher, Louise 121
The Flintstones (1994) 156
Flowers in the Attic (1987) 121
Flynn, Errol 58, 183, 184, 201
Follow the Boys (1944) 260
Fonda, Henry 199
For the Future: The Irvine Fertility Scandal (1996) 75
The Forbidden Dance (1990) 111

Ford, John 193
The Foreign Affair (novel) 145
Foreign Correspondent (1940) 104
Forest Lawn Memorial Park–Glendale 57, 58
Forman, Carol 54
Forrest, Frederic 67
Forrest Gump (1994) 250
Forsythe, John 119
Fort Apache (1948) 193
Fort Roach 47, 49
48 HRS. (1982) 72
Foster, Preston 51
4th Street Viaduct 23, 26, **28**, 29, 31, 212, **213**, **241**, 242, 243
Fox, Michael J. 36, 226
Fox, Virginia 18
Fox, William 140
Fox Film Corp. 140
Franciosa, Anthony 133
Frankenstein (1931) 141
Friends 'till the End (1997) 157
Front Page (TV) 38
Frye, Dwight 51
Fuller, Penny 69
Fuller, Robert 55
"Fun Factory" 138
Fury of the Congo (1951) 155

Gable, Clark 36, 127, 183
Gable, John Clark 36
Garcia, Andy 73
Garland, Judy 129
Garner, James 29, 31, 79, 94
Garr, Teri 32
Garth, Jennie 67
General Hospital (TV) 93, **95**
Georgia Street Receiving Hospital 98
Gere, Richard 73
Get Out of Town (1962) 71
Getty, Estelle 25, 243
Gibson, Mel 153
Gibson, Thomas 121
Glen Island Casino 164
Glendale-Hyperion Viaduct (Bridge) 23, 32, **33**
The Glenn Miller Story (1954) 13, 162, 163, **165**, 179, 233
Gless, Sharon 79
Glover, Danny 38, 153, 242
The Gold Rush (1925) 198
Goldman, Ron 38, 176
Gone with the Wind (1939) 127
Gone with the Wind (novel) 36

The Good Earth (1937) 199
Good Samaritan Hospital 98
Goodman, John 156
Goodyear Tire and Rubber Plant (site) 34, 44, **45**
Gosselaar, Mark-Paul 238
Gould, Elliott 73
Grable, Betty 9
Grammer, Kelsey 98
Grand Central Airport 5, 6, 7
Grand Central Market 38
Grant, Cary 219
Grant/Tinker Gannett Studios 127
Grauman, Sid 247
Grayson, Kathryn 16, 129
Greedy (1994) 36
Grey, Virginia 193, 195
Greystone Mansion 117, **120**, 121, **122**, 123
Griffith, Andy 113, 201, 202
Griffith, Griffith J. 144
Griffith, Melanie 236
Griffith Observatory 144, **146**, 148, 150
Griffith Park 50, 56, 144, 149, 150
Grogan, Bob 82, 172
Gross, Michael 53
Gumble, Bryant 103
Guttenberg, Steven 268

Hadley, Reed 137
Hal Roach Studios 46, **47**, **48**, 49, 64, 123, 124, 135, **136**, 137, 267
Hale, Alan 51
Hall, Philip Baker 42
Hall of Justice 81, 84, **85**, **86**, 87
Halliday, John 236
Hamilton, George 173
Hamilton, Linda 37, 77, 171, 263
Hammett, Dashiel 101
Hanks, Tom 250
Hanna, William 156
Hardy, Oliver 3, 44, 45, 46, 136, 205, 207, 208, 235
The Hardy Boys/Nancy Drew Mysteries (TV) 108
Harlow (1965) 184
Harlow, Jean 184, 19
Harrison, Gregory 251
Harry Chandler Rancho Santa Anita, Inc. 150
Harry O (TV) 108
Harvard University 54
Hatcher, Mary 133, 249
Hatton, Raymond 7
Hauer, Rutger 213, 214, 243, 270

Havers, Nigel 107
Hayes, George "Gabby" 155
Hearst, Patty 84
Hearst, William Randolph 128
Heart of the City (TV) 267
Heartbreakers (1984) 263
Heavenly Days (1944) 9
Hedren, Tippi 236
Hell's Angels (1930) 198
Henner, Marilu 75, 102
Henstridge, Natasha 167, 189
Her Last Chance (1996) 145
Here Comes the Navy (1934) 257, **258**, 260
Herman, Jerry 104
Hero (1992) 73
Herring, Laura 111
Herrmann, Edward 105
Heston, Charlton 198
High and Dizzy (1920) 267
Highland Park (Northeast) Police Station 168, **169**, 170
Hill Street Tunnel 267
Hit the Ice (1943) **141**, 143
Hitchcock, Alfred 102, 104, 170, 222
Hoffman, Dustin 73, 128
Hold Back the Dawn (1941) 94
Holden, William 259
Hollywood Boulevard 234, 236, **237**, 238, 249, 250, 251
Hollywood Boulevard (1936) 236
Hollywood Bowl 15, **16**
Hollywood Lake (Lake Hollywood) 210, 211
Hollywood Memorial Park Cemetery 57, 58, **59**, **60**, **61**, **62**, **63**, 187
Hollywood Reservoir 209, **210**, 211
Hollywood Subway Station 251
Holt, Tim 51, 201
Hood, Darla 59, **61**, 116
Hook (1991) 128
Hopalong Cassidy (TV) 202
Hope, Bob 193
Hopetown 193
Hopeville 193
Hopper, Dennis 74, 151, 230, 245, 246
Hot Moves (1984) 162
House of Frankenstein 1997 (1997) 145
A House of Secrets and Lies (1992) 91
Houseman, John 118
Houston, Whitney 73
Howland Island 35
Hudson, Rochelle 186
Huffman, Felicity 209
Hughes, Carol 147

Hughes, Frank John 78, 148
Hughes, Howard 198
Hull, Henry 154
Hunt, Marsha 236
Huston, Virginia 114
Huston Walter 103, 201
Hutchins, Bobby "Wheezer" 123
Hutton, Betty 133, 259
Huxley, Aldous 246
Hymer, Warren 186

I Love Lucy (TV) 131, 251
Ice-T 78
In Society (1944) 32
In the Line of Duty: Kidnapped (1995) 27, 243
In the Navy (1941) **258**, **259**
In the Shadows: Someone's Watching (1993) 224
Independence Day (1996) 29, 265
The Indestructible Man (1956) 35, 84, 180, 233
Indian Head Rock 197, 199, **200**, 201
The Inheritance (1997) 121
The Innocent (1994) 98
An Innocent Man (1989) 27
The Invaders (1995) 26, 98, 102, 157, 170, 189
Irving Thalberg Building 129, **131**, 132
It's a Wonderful Life (1946) 219, **221**
It's Nothing Personal (1993) 74, 88
Iturbi, Jose 15, 16, 129
Iverson Ranch 55, 192, 197, **200**, 202, 203, 207, 215, 217

The Jack Benny Program (TV) 190
Jack Reed: Badge of Honor (1993) 102
Jack the Ripper 264
Jack's Back (1988) 264
Jackson, Michael 253
The Jacksons: An American Dream (1992) 253
Jake and the Fatman (TV) 267
Jericho Fever (1993) 102
Jesus Christ 198
Jillian, Ann 29
Johnson, Chic 237
Johnson, Don 84
Jones, Allan 200
Jones, Carolyn 133
Jones, Tommy Lee 107
Jungle Jim (TV) 195
Jungle Jim (1948) 155, 193
Jury of One (1992) 83

Kane, "Babe" 184, 185
Kaufman, Andy 21
Kaye, Darwood "Waldo" 116
Keaton, Buster 118, 197
Keaton, Diane 35
Keaton, Michael 236
Kelly, Gene 15, 16, 129, 195, 249, 250
Kelly, Nancy 200
Kelman, Judith 224
Kennedy, Arthur 49
Kennedy, John F. (U.S. president) 19
Kennedy, Robert F. (U.S. senator) 80, 98, 99
The Kennedys 189
Kern, Jerome 129
Kerns, Joanna 74, 87
Kibbee, Guy 49
Kidder, Margot 191
Kidnapped (1987) 161
Kids Don't Tell (1985) 160
Kilmer, Val 107
King, Martin Luther, Jr. 80
King, Perry 102
King Kong (1933) 128
King of Kings (1927) 247
Kinski, Natassja 76
Kline, Kevin 113
Kojak (TV) 78
Kramer, Stephanie 67
Kristofferson, Kris 181
Kung Fu (1972) 155

L.A. Confidential (1997) 76
L.A. Law (TV) 83, 92, 140
L.A. Story (1991) 269
La Bamba (1987) 253
Ladd, Cheryl 166
Lady Killer (1933) 7, 185
Laemmle, Carl 140
Lake, Arthur 137, 187
Lakeside Country Club 115, 116
Lakeside Golf Club of Hollywood 115
Lamour, Dorothy 259
Land and Live in the Desert (1943) 49
Landis, Carole 200
Land's End (TV) 78, 174
Langan, Glenn 144
Lansburg, G. Albert 17
Lansbury, Angela 56, 67, 123
Lassie (TV) 157
The Last Action Hero (1993) 26
The Last Days of Pompeii (1935) 51
Laurel, Stan 3, 44, 45, 46, 136, 205, 207, 208, 235

Lawler, Jerry 21
Lawrence, Martin 75
Lawrence, Rosina 205, 107
Learn to Live (1943) 49
LeBaron, Ervil 85
Leffert, General 44
Leigh, Janet 141
Leigh, Vivien 36, 127
Lemmon, Jack 107, 108
Lethal Weapon 3 (1992) 153, 239
The Letter (1982) 110
Lewinski, Monica 219
Lewis, Geoffrey 78
Lewis, Jerry 261
Lewis, Sinclair 103
Liar, Liar (1997) 77
The Life and Legend of Wyatt Earp (TV) 206
Light, Judith 97
Light Rail–Metro Rail Maintenance Facility 24, 184
Lightning (novel) 265
Lindsay, Margaret 7
Lithgow, John 73
Little, Clevon 155
Little Bighorn River 201
The Lives of a Bengal Lancer (1935) 198
Livingston, Mary 190
Livingston, Robert 53
Lloyd, Harold 46, 267
The Lone Ranger (movie) (1956) 51
The Lone Ranger (serial) (1938) 204
The Lone Ranger (TV) 55
The Lone Ranger Rides Again (serial) (1939) 53
Long, Shelley 67
Look Out Below (1918) 267
Lopez, Jennifer 114
Lord of the Flies (1990) 111
Los Angeles Central Receiving Hospital 93, 98, 99
Los Angeles City Hall 66, 69, 70, 71, 76, 80
Los Angeles County District Attorney 82
Los Angeles County Fire Department 55
Los Angeles County General Hospital 93
Los Angeles County Municipal Court Building 93, 95, 97
Los Angeles International Airport (LAX) 5, 6
Los Angeles Metropolitan Airport 5, 6, 7, 8, 10

280   INDEX

Los Angeles MTA Subway 244, **245**
Los Angeles Police (Department) 32, 37, 38, 75, 168, 173, 238, 264
Los Angeles Police Academy 168, 170, **171**, 172
Los Angeles Police Historical Society Museum 169
Los Angeles Riot (1992) 172
Los Angeles River 23, 30, 31, 32, 212, 213, 269, **270, 271**
Los Angeles Valley College 218, **222**, 223
Loughlin, Lori 181
A Love Affair: The Eleanor and Lou Gehrig Story (1978) 105
Love Can Be Murder (1992) 145
Loy, Myrna 219
Lupino, Ida 70
LuPone, Patti 145
Lyons, Phyllis 165

McArthur, Alex 32, 265
MacArthur Park 246
McBain, Ed 265
MacCorkindale, Simon 160
McCrea, Joel 104, 206
McCullough, Colleen 79
McDonald, Christopher 71
MacDonald, Jeanette 57, **58**, 183
MacDonald, Ross 145
McFarland, George "Spanky" 116
MacGyver (TV) 108
McKean, Michael 263
McLaglen, Victor 199
McNamara, William 107
McRaney, Gerald 170
Madonna 111
Madsen, Virginia 162
Major Dad (TV) 170
Malamud, Bernard 106
Malden, Karl 172
Mame (1974) 104
The Man from Oklahoma (1945) 155
Mancuso, Nick 263
Mandylor, Costas 78
Mann's (Grauman's) Chinese Theater 247, **248**, 249, 251
Manson, Charles 87
Manson Family **86**, 87
Mantooth, Randolph 55
Marina Del Rey 159, **160, 161**
Marina Del Rey Channel 160
Mariner's Statue 160, **161**
Marshall High School 218, 223, **224**, 225

Martin, Dean 133, 261
Martin, Kellie 145
Martin, Steve 269
Marx Brothers (Groucho, Chico, Harpo and Zeppo) 118
The Mask (1994) 31, **40**, 41
Matheson, Tim 29, 74, 209, 210
Matthau, Walter 107, 108
Mature, Victor 200
Media Park 149
Meet Danny Wilson (1952) 104
Meet the Applegates (1991) 111
Melody Ranch 192, 204, **205**, 207
Men Don't Tell (1993) 97, 228, **229**, 230
Menendez, Erik 236
Menendez, Lyle 236
Menendez: A Killing in Beverly Hills (1994) 236
Meredith, Burgess 137
Mexicali Rose (1939) 206
M-G-M School 218, **225**, 226
M-G-M Studios 124, 129, **130, 131**, 132, 225
Middleton, Charles 147
Midler, Bette 22
Midnight Run (1988) 72
Midnight's Child (1992) 223
Milano, Alyssa 165
Miller, Glenn 233
Millican, James 235
Mimieux, Yvette 160
Miranda, Carmen 9
Mitchell, Margaret 36
Mitchum, Robert 104, 106
Modine, Matthew 236
Mogelberg, George 70
Money Talks (1997) 26, 265
Monti, Carlotta 104
Moore, Clayton 51, 55
Moore, Demi 263
Moore, Dennis 147
Moore, Dudley 22
Moore, Victor 133
Moranis, Rick 156
Morgan, Dennis 181
Morgan, Harry 14, 162, 180
Moss, Jerry 127
Moulton, Charles 56
Mt. Vesuvius 51
Mulgrew, Kate 223
Mulholland, William 211
Mulholland Dam 211
Mulholland Falls (1996) 75
The Mummy (1932) 141

INDEX 281

Muni, Paul 199
Murder Between Friends (1994) 74
Murder in the First (1995) 37
Murder One (TV) 83, 174
Murder, She Wrote (TV) 55, 67, 95, 108, 122, 175
Murphy, Eddie 67, 72, 84, 166
The Music Box (1932) 3

The Naked Gun: From the Files of Police Squad (1988) 27, 72, 241, 269
Naked Gun 33½: The Final Insult (1994) 19, 89
National Hotel 43
The Natural (1984) 106
Naughton, David 161
Naval Training Center (NTC) (San Diego) 256, **257**, **258**, **259**, **260**, 261
Neal, Patricia 202
Neeson, Liam 268
Ness, Eliot 80, 271
The Net (1995) 163
Never Give a Sucker an Even Break (1941) 33
Newbern, George 270
Nicholson, Jack 36, 72
Nielsen, Leslie 19, 27, 72, 113
Night Has a Thousand Eyes (1948) 179, 232
The Night Stalker (TV) 108
The Night That Panicked America (1975) 263
Nightmare (1991) 223
Nimoy, Leonard 246
Nixon, Richard M. (U.S. president) 227, 250
Nolan, Lloyd 49
Nolte, Nick 72, 75, 111
Norris, Edward 186
Nouri, Michael 266
Novak, Kim 102
Novarro, Ramon 198

O'Brien, Austin 26
O'Brien, Hugh 207
O'Brien, Pat 257
Obsessive Love (1984) 160
O'Connell, Jerry 158
O'Connor, Donald 249, 250
O'Donnell, Chris 107
Of Mice and Men (1939) 137
The Oklahoma Kid (1939) 199
Olsen, Ole 237
Olvera, Agustin 238

Olvera Street 153, 234, 238, **239**, **240**
Olympic Auditorium 17, 19, **20**, 21
Olympic Games (1932) 238
Olympic Village (1932) 238
On the Line (1998) 37, 77, 171, 265
Once You Meet a Stranger (1996) 170, 189
One Dark Night (1983) 263
One Million B.C. (1939) 200
One Night in the Tropics (1940) 200
One Woman's Courage (1994) 74
Ontkean, Michael 160
Ororati, Peter 36
Our Gang 46, 59, 61, 115, 116, 123, 226
Out to Sea (1997) 107
Outside the Wall (1950) 70

Pacific Heights (1990) 236
Pangborn, Franklin 185
Paramount Pictures (Studios) 124, 132, 133, **134**
Parker, Corey 107
Parker, Jameson 166
Parker, William H. 172
Parker Center Police Headquarters 168, 172, **173**, **174**, **175**, 176
Pasadena Civic Auditorium 17, **22**
Pasadena Train Station (Depot) 177, **183**, 184
Pathé Studios 127
Payne, John 187
Penn, Sean 230
Perfect Alibi (1994) 32
Perkins, Anthony 141
Perkins, Elizabeth 156
Perrine, Valerie 104
Pershing Square Park **101**, 149, 150, **151**, 244, 246
Pershing Square Subway Station 151, 245
Peter Pan 128
Pfeiffer, Michelle 36
The Phantom (1996) 113
The Phil Silvers Show (TV) 135
Philips, Gina 128
Phillips, Michelle 182
Pico House 34, **43**, 44
Placerita Canyon State Park 149, 153, 192, 207, **208**
Players (TV) 78, 148
The Plaza (Pueblo de Los Angeles Plaza) 240
Plaza Park 43, 44, 149, **152**, 153, 154, 239, 240
Poitier, Sidney 264
Police Academy (1984) 268

Police Academy 2: Their First Assignment (1985) 268
Police Academy 6: City Under Siege (1989) 26, 169, 242
Police Administration Building 172
Police Story: The Freeway Killings (1987) 264
Police Squad (TV) 27, 72
Police Woman (TV) 108
Pollack, Ben 162, 164
Polo, Marco 199
P.O.W. The Escape (1986) 110
Powell, Dick 258, 259
Powell, Lee 204
Power, Tyrone 61
Preble Parade Field 257, **258**, **259**, 260, 261
Predator (1987) 38
Predator 2 (1990) 38, 242, 244
Prehistoric Jungle Garden 114
Presley, Elvis 31, 250
Presley, Priscilla 19
Preston, Robert 104
The Pretender (TV) 79
Price, Vincent 195
The Price of Love (1995) 251
Priestley, Jason 77
Principal, Victoria 223
Profiler (TV) 190
Prophet of Evil: The Ervil LeBaron Story (1993) 85
Pryor, Richard 237
Psycho (1960) 141, **142**
Pueblo de Los Angeles Plaza *see* The Plaza
Pullman, Bill 29
The Purple Monster Strikes (serial) (1945) 147

Quaid, Randy 265
Quantum Leap (TV) 108
Queen Anne Cottage 181
Queen Mary 100, 103, **105**, **106**, 108
Queen of Angels Hospital 93, 96, 97, 98
Queen of England 27
Quicksand: No Escape (1991) 209
Quiet on the Set (book) 197
Quincy, M.E. (TV) 108
Quinn, Anthony 201

Race Against Time: The Search for Sarah (1996) 33, 254
Racket Squad (TV) 137
Raft, George 260

Rainer, Luise 199
Ralston, Esther 236
Ramsey, Anne 222
Range Busters 193
Rathbone, Basil 199, 237
Raymond, Alex 193
Read, James 191
Reagan, Ron 38
Reagan, Ronald (U.S. president) 38, 47
Recruit Training Command (RTC) 256
Redford, Robert 106, 264
Reed, Shanna 170
Reeves, Keanu 74, 151, 245, 246, 250, 251
Remick, Lee 110, 202
Renaldo, Duncan 202
Reno, Kelly 44, 154
Rescue Me (1993) 166, 210
Resisting Enemy Interrogation (1943) 49
Reynolds, Burt 103, 110
Reynolds, Debbie 249
Rice, Florence 29
Ricochet (1991) 73
Riders of Destiny (1933) 204
Rin Tin Tin 196
Rin Tin Tin (TV) 196
Ritter, John 110
R.K.O. Radio Pictures 127, 132, 193
Roach, Hal 47, 115, 123
Robinson, Edward G. 179, 232
The Rockford Files (TV) 29, 79
The Rockford Files: Friends and Foul Play (1996) 94, 171
The Rockford Files: I Still Love L.A. (1994) 79
The Rockford Files: If the Frame Fits (1996) 29
Rocky (1976) 3
Rogers, Jean 146
Rogers, Mimi 73
Rogers, Roy 155, 202
Rogers, Will 140, 183
Rogers St. Johns, Adela 249
Romero, Cesar 199
The Rookies (TV) 108
Rooney, Mickey 130
Rose Bowl 22
Rose Parade 22
Ross Cutlery 38
Rossini, Gioacchino 55
The Roy Rogers Show (TV) 202
Ruman, Sig 14, 16, 180
Russell, Gail 179
Russell, Theresa 170

Sadler, William 102
Sagebrush Trail (1933) 50
Sahara (1943) 201
Sailor Beware (1951) 259, 261
St. Brendan's Church 64, **65**
St. Francis Dam 211
St. Ives (1976) 118
San Juan, Olga 133, 249
Sandford, Stanley "Tiny" 44
Santa Anita Depot 177, 181, **182**
Santa Fe Avenue 24, 25, 26, 27, 29, 31, 32, 214, 234, 240, **241**, 242, 243, 269, 271
Santa Fe Railroad Station 24, 25, 177, 184, **185**, **186**, 187
Santa Fe Railroad Tracks 240
Santa Monica Ballroom 162, 163, 164, **165**
Santa Monica Elks Lodge 136
Santa Monica Pier 159, 162, **163**, 167
Santa Monica Pier Electric Car Ride 162, 163, **164**, 165
Santa Monica Pier Merry-Go-Round 162, 163, 166
Santa Monica Pier Parking Area 166, 167
Santa Susana Pass Road 215, **216**, 217
Savalas, Telly 78
Scalia, Jack 165
Scene of the Crime (TV) **182**
Schenck, Joseph 139
Schwarznegger, Arnold 26, 75, 111, 250, 263
Scott, Gordon 114
seaQuest DSV (TV) 108
The Searchers (1956) 53
The Second Hundered Years (1927) 44, **45**
2nd Street Tunnel 12, 14, 262, **266**, 267
Sellecca, Connie 91, 251
Selleck, Tom 27
Selznick International Pictures 127
Sennett, Mack 127, 138, 184
Sennett Studios (Mack Sennett Studios) 124, **138**
749 E. Temple Street Building 41, 42, 43
7th Street Viaduct 240
77th Bengal Lancers (TV) 157
Shameful Secrets (1993) 74
Shannon, Frank 147
Shaw, C. Montague 203
Shayne, Cari 121
Sheen, Charlie 26
Shell Game (TV) 191
Shenar, Paul 263
Sherman, Lowell 249

Sherman, Robert G. 197
Short, Martin 111
Show Them No Mercy (1935) 186
Shrine Auditorium 17, **18**, 19
Sidney, Silvia 199
Siegel, Benjamin "Bugsy" 72
Sierra Madre Town Square 254, **255**
Sightings (TV) 108
Silbar, Adam 162
Silverheels, Jay 51, 55
Silvers, Phil 135
Silverstone, Alicia 107, 225
Simpson, Orenthal James 38, 83, 84, **175**
Sinatra (1992) 189
Sinatra, Frank 15, 16, 104, 129, 189
Singin' in the Rain (1952) 249
Singleton, Penny 187
6th Street Viaduct 23, **30**, 31, 32, 212, 213, 214, 243, 269, **270**, 271
Slater, Christian 37
Sliders (TV) 158
Small Talk (1929) 123
Smart, J. Scott 101
Smith, Bubba 27, 268
Smith, C. Aubrey 199
Smith, Jaclyn 145
Smith, Howard 135
Smith, Kent 49
Smith, Leon 2, 165
Smith, Will 29
Smits, Jimmy 94
Snapdragon (1993) 97
Sneakers (1992) 264
Sometimes They Come Back (1991) 53
Sometimes They Come Back … Again (1996) 53
Sons of the Desert (1933) 136
Sony Corporation/Columbia Studios 129
Spacey, Kevin 77
Spade Cooley Show (TV) 164
Species (1995) 166, 189
Speed (1994) 74, **151**, 245, 250
Spenser, John 83
Spring Street Towers 34, 40, 41
Spy Hard (1996) 113
Stack, Robert 65
Stallone, Sylvester 25, 243
Stamos, John 265
Stanwyck, Barbara 181
Star Dust (1940) 184, 187, 249
A Star Is Born (1937) 249
A Star Is Born (1954) 249
A Star Is Born (1976) 249
Star Spangled Rhythm (1942) 133, 259

284   INDEX

Steiger, Rod 104
Steinbeck, John 137
Stevens, Warren 157
Stewart, Catherine Mary 264
Stewart, James 14, 102, 162, 164, 180, 233
Stick (1985) 110
Stockwell, Dean 98
Stop! Or My Mom Will Shoot (1992) 25, 242, 243
Strangers on a Train (1951) 170, 222
Strauss, Peter 97, 144, 230
Strike Me Pink (1936) 9
Stuart, Gloria 257
Sundown (1941) 51
Superman (serial) (1948) 54
Sutherland, Donald 134, 209, 210
Sutherland, Kiefer 42, 75
Swank, Hilary 87
Switch (TV) 108
Switzer, Carl "Alfalfa" 59, 116
Swope Park 150

Tagget (1991) 219
Tarzan 193, 195
Tarzan and the Slave Girl (1950) 114
Tarzan's Hidden Jungle (1955) 114
Tarzan's Lagoon **112**, 113, 114
Tarzan's Peril (1951) 114
Taylor, Elizabeth 107, 135, 156, 201, 226
Tell Me No Secrets (1997) 180, 181
Temple, Shirley 140, 199, 219
"10" (1979) 21, 22
Tennant, Victoria 121
The Terminator (1984) 263
Terminator 2: Judgement Day (1991) 111
Terror in the Family (1996) 87
That's Entertainment (1947) 130
Them! (1954) 32, 269
Them! Tunnel 214, 243, 262, 269, **270**, 271
There Must Be a Pony (1986) 135
They Died With Their Boots On (1941) 201
A Thin Line Between Love and Hate (1996) 75
3rd Street Tunnel 12, 13, 14, **178**, 181, 231, 232, 233, 262, 267, **268**, 269
This Man's Navy (1945) **10**, 11
Thomas H. Ince Studios 127
The Thorn Birds (TV) 79
The Three Ages (1923) 197
Three Fugitives (1923) 111
Three Men in a Tub (1939) 116
"Three Mesquiteers" 193
The Three Musketeers (1948) 195

Throw Momma from the Train (1987) 222
Thunder Cloud, Chief 53, 204
Tierney, Gene 51
Tighe, Kevin 55
Till the Clouds Roll By (1946) 129
Tilly, Meg 263
Todd, Mike 107
Todd, Thelma 73
Todd Pacific Shipyards Corporation 228, 229, 230
Toluca Lake 109, **115**, 116
Toma (TV) 108
Tombstone Epitaph (newspaper) 206
Tombstone Territory (TV) 206
Tone, Franchot 198
Tracy, Spencer 58
The Trail of the Lonesome Pine (1936) 198
Travanti, Daniel J. 219
Travis, Colonel 44
Treacherous Crossing (1992) 106
The Treasure of the Sierra Madre (1948) 201
The Trials of Rose O'Neill (TV) 79
Troop Beverly Hills (1989) 67
True Crime (1996) 225
Tucker, Chris 26
Tucker, Sophie 260
Tumbling Tumbleweeds (1935) 204
Turner, Lana 195, 199
Turturro, John 72
Tustin U.S. Marine Corps Air Station 5, **10**, 11
20th Century–Fox Studios 124, **139**, 140
Twentieth Century Pictures 139
The Twilight Zone (TV) 31
Twin Sisters (1992) 67
Twins (1988) 250
The Two Jakes (1990) 72

Undersea Kingdom (Serial) (1936) 203
Underwood, Blair 266
Union Passenger Terminal 187
Union Station 24, 177, 184, 187, **188**, 189, 190, 191, 244, **245**, 246
United States Government District Court Building 81, **90**, 91, 92
Universal City 32, 140
Universal Film Manufacturing Company 140
Universal Pictures Studios (Universal Studios) 32, 47, 115, 124, 140, **141**, 142, 143, 191, 237
Unnatural Causes (1986) 110

Unsolved Mysteries (TV) 62, 65, 80, 108, 271
U.S.C. (University of Southern California) 19

"*V*" (1983) 53
V: The Final Battle (1984) 53
Valens, Ritchie 253
Valentino, Rudolph 61, **63**, 187
The Vampire Bat (1933) 51
Van Ark, Joan 224
Van Nuys Airport 7, **8**
Variety Girl (1947) 133, 249
Vasquez Rocks County Park 149, 154, **156**, 158
Vendetta (1950) 195
Verdugo, Elena 206
Vertigo (1955) 102
Victim of Love (1991) 162, 166
Vine Street 238
The Virginian (1946) 206
Virtuosity (1995) 20, 61
Vital Signs (1990) 94

Wagner, Lindsay 106
Wagner, Robert 135
Walker, Ally 190
Walker, Frank 207
Walker, Marcy 223
Walker, Robert 129
Walker Ranch 207
Wambaugh, Joseph 83
The War of the Worlds (1953) 65
The War of the Worlds (Novel) 263
Ward, Rachel 79
Warner Bros. (Studios) 115, 139
Washington, Denzel 20, 61, 73, 145
Way Out West (1937) **205**, 207, **208**
Wayne, John 50, 53, 193, 204
W.C. Fields and Me (1976) 104
Webb, Jack 172
Wedlock (1991) 213, 243, 269
Wee Willie Winkie (1937) 199
Weiss, Michael T. 79
Weissmuller, Johnny 155, 193, 195
Welles, Orson 128, 182, 263
Wells, H.G. 263
Werewolf of London (1935) 154

West, Mae 183
West, Nathanael 134
What Price Hollywood? (1932) 249
While the City Sleeps (1928) 69
While the City Sleeps (1956) 70
White Hot: The Mysterious Murder of Thelma Todd (1991) 73
Whittier High School 218, **226**, 227
Who's That Girl? (1987) 111
Wild Palms (TV) 80
Wilder, Gene 237
Wilder, James 29, 87
Wilding, Michael 107
"William Tell Overture" 55
Williams, JoBeth 162
Williams, Robin 76, 128
Willis, Bruce 72
Wills, Chill 205
Wilson, Don 190
Wilson, Douglas 71
Wiltern Theater 247, 251, **252**, 253
The Winds of War (1983) 105
Wine Street 238
Wise, Ray 107
Wister, Owen 206
Wolf (1994) 36
Won Ton Ton, the Dog Who Saved Hollywood (1976) 134, 250
Wonder Woman (TV) 56
Wood, Natalie 53
Woodard, Alfre 110
Woods, James 71
Wouk, Herman 105
Wyatt Earp (TV) 206

Yeats-Brown, Francis 198
Young, Chic 137
Young, Roland 187
Young, Sean 263
The Young and the Restless (TV) 108
Young Doctors in Love (1982) 263

Zane, Billy 82, 94, 113, 264
Zanuck, Darryl F. 139
Zapped (1982) 223
Zimbalist, Stephanie 102
Zorek, Michael 162
Zorro Rides Again (serial) (1937) 203

www.ingramcontent.com/pod-product-compliance
Lightning Source LLC
Chambersburg PA
CBHW051211300426
44116CB00006B/522